The
GREATEST
Sermons
EVER
PREACHED

The
GREATEST
Sermons
EVER
PREACHED

COMPILED BY
TRACEY D. LAWRENCE

W PUBLISHING GROUP
A Division of Thomas Nelson Publishers
Since 1798

www.wpublishinggroup.com

Published by W Publishing Group, a Division of Thomas Nelson, Inc., P.O. Box 141000, Nashville, Tennessee 37214.

Scripture quotations noted KJV are from the King James Version.

Scripture quotations noted NIV are from the Holy Bible, New International Version. Copyright © 1973, 1978, 1984, International Bible Society. Used by permission of Zondervan.

The New Revised Standard Version Bible (NRSV), copyright © 1989 by the Division of Christian Education of the National Council of the Churches of Christ in the USA.

The Holy Bible, New Century Version (NCV), copyright © 1987, 1988, 1991 by Word Publishing, a division of Thomas Nelson, Inc. Used by permission.

Scripture quotations noted NKJV are from The New King James Version, copyright © 1979, 1980, 1982, Thomas Nelson, Inc., Publishers.

Library of Congress Cataloging-in-Publication Data

Printed in the United States of America

05 06 07 08 09 QW 9 8 7 6 5 4 3 2 1

CONTENTS

Contents

1

Abraham Lincoln

SECOND INAUGURAL ADDRESS

─────

Abraham Lincoln (1809–1865) was the sixteenth president of the United States (1861–1865). The spirit that guided his presidency was articulated in his Second Inaugural Address, which was delivered March 4, 1865.

Fellow Countrymen:

At this second appearing to take the oath of the presidential office, there is less occasion for an extended address than there was at the first. Then a statement somewhat in detail of a course to be pursued seemed fitting and proper. Now, at the expiration of four years, during which public declarations have been constantly called forth on every point and phase of the great contest which still absorbs the attention and engrosses the energies of the nation, little that is new could be presented. The progress of our arms, upon which all else chiefly depends, is as well known to the public as to myself, and it is, I trust, reasonably satisfactory and encouraging to all. With high hope for the future, no prediction in regard to it is ventured.

On the occasion corresponding to this four years ago, all thoughts were anxiously directed to an impending civil war. All dreaded it; all sought to avert it. While the inaugural address was being delivered from this place, devoted altogether to *saving* the Union without war, urgent agents were in the city seeking to *destroy* it without war—seeking to dissolve the Union and divide effects by negotiation. Both parties deprecated war, but one of them would *make* war rather than let the nation survive, and the other would *accept* war rather than let it perish, and the war came.

One-eighth of the whole population were colored slaves, not distributed generally over the Union, but localized in the southern part of it. These slaves constituted a peculiar and powerful interest. All knew that this interest was somehow the cause of the war. To strengthen, perpetuate, and extend this interest was the object for which the insurgents would rend the Union even by war, while the government claimed no right to do more than to restrict the territorial enlargement of it. Neither party expected for the war the magnitude or the duration which it has already attained. Neither anticipated that the *cause* of the conflict might cease with or even before the conflict itself should cease. Each looked for an easier triumph, and a result less fundamental and astounding. Both read the same Bible and pray to the same God, and each invokes His aid against the other. It may seem strange that any men should dare to ask a just God's assistance in wringing their bread from the sweat of other men's faces, but let us judge not, that we be not judged. The prayers of both could not be answered. That of neither has been answered fully. The Almighty has His own purposes. "Woe unto the world because of offences! for it must needs be that offences come; but woe to that man by whom the offence cometh!" [Matthew 18:7 KJV]. If we shall suppose that American slavery is one of those offenses which, in the providence of God, must needs come, but which, having continued through His appointed time, He now wills to remove, and that He gives to both North and South this terrible war as the woe due to those by whom the offense came, shall we discern therein any departure from those divine attributes which the believers in a living God always ascribe to Him? Fondly do we hope, fervently do we pray, that this mighty scourge of war may speedily pass away. Yet if God wills that it continue until all the wealth piled by the bondsman's two hundred and fifty years of unrequited toil shall be sunk, and until every drop of blood drawn with the lash shall be paid by another drawn with the sword, as was said three thousand years ago, so still it must be said, "The judgments of the LORD are true and righteous altogether" [Psalm 19:9 KJV].

With malice toward none, with charity for all, with firmness in the right as God gives us to see the right, let us strive on to finish the work we are in, to bind up the nation's wounds, to care for him who shall have borne the battle and for his widow and his orphan, to do all which may achieve and cherish a just and lasting peace among ourselves and with all nations.

This sermon is in the public domain.

The Prophet Ezekiel

IRRESPONSIBLE SHEPHERDS

Ezekiel lived during 600 BC, a time of great international upheaval. He was among the Jews exiled to Babylon by Nebuchadnezzar. While among the exiles, he received his calling from God to become a prophet.

EZEKIEL 34:1–10

And the word of the LORD came to me, saying, "Son of man, prophesy against the shepherds of Israel, prophesy and say to them, 'Thus says the Lord GOD to the shepherds: "Woe to the shepherds of Israel who feed themselves! Should not the shepherds feed the flocks? You eat the fat and clothe yourselves with the wool; you slaughter the fatlings, but you do not feed the flock. The weak you have not strengthened, nor have you healed those who were sick, nor bound up the broken, nor brought back what was driven away, nor sought what was lost; but with force and cruelty you have ruled them. So they were scattered because there was no shepherd; and they became food for all the beasts of the field when they were scattered. My sheep wandered through all the mountains, and on every high hill; yes, My flock was scattered over the whole face of the earth, and no one was seeking or searching for them."

"'Therefore, you shepherds, hear the word of the LORD: "As I live," says the Lord GOD, "surely because My flock became a prey, and My flock became food for every beast of the field, because there was no shepherd, nor did My shepherds search for My flock, but the shepherds fed themselves and did not feed My flock"—therefore, O shepherds, hear the word of the LORD!

"'Thus says the Lord GOD: "Behold, I am against the shepherds, and I will require My flock at their hand; I will cause them to cease feeding the sheep, and the shepherds shall feed themselves no more; for I will deliver My flock from their mouths, that they may no longer be food for them."'"

GOD, THE TRUE SHEPHERD (VV. 11–31)

"'For thus says the Lord GOD: "Indeed I Myself will search for My sheep and seek them out. As a shepherd seeks out his flock on the day he is among his scattered sheep, so will I seek out My sheep and deliver them from all the places where they were scattered on a cloudy and dark day. And I will bring them out from the peoples and gather them from the countries, and will bring them to their own land; I will feed them on the mountains of Israel, in the valleys and in all the inhabited places of the country. I will feed them in good pasture, and their fold shall be on the high mountains of Israel. There they shall lie down in a good fold and feed in rich pasture on the mountains of Israel. I will feed My flock, and I will make them lie down," says the Lord GOD. "I will seek what was lost and bring back what was driven away, bind up the broken and strengthen what was sick; but I will destroy the fat and the strong, and feed them in judgment."

"'And as for you, O My flock, thus says the Lord GOD: "Behold, I shall judge between sheep and sheep, between rams and goats. Is it too little for you to have eaten up the good pasture, that you must tread down with your feet the residue of your pasture—and to have drunk of the clear waters, that you must foul the residue with your feet? And as for My flock, they eat what you have trampled with your feet, and they drink what you have fouled with your feet."

"'Therefore thus says the Lord GOD to them: "Behold, I Myself will judge between the fat and the lean sheep. Because you have pushed with side and shoulder, butted all the weak ones with your horns, and scattered them abroad, therefore I will save My flock, and they shall no longer be a prey; and I will judge between sheep and sheep. I will establish one shepherd over them, and he shall feed them—My servant David. He shall feed them and be their shepherd. And I, the LORD, will be their God, and My servant David a prince among them; I, the LORD, have spoken.

"'"I will make a covenant of peace with them, and cause wild beasts to cease from the land; and they will dwell safely in the wilderness and sleep in the woods. I will make them and the places all around My hill a blessing; and I will cause showers to come down in their season; there shall be showers of blessing.

Then the trees of the field shall yield their fruit, and the earth shall yield her increase. They shall be safe in their land; and they shall know that I am the LORD, when I have broken the bands of their yoke and delivered them from the hand of those who enslaved them. And they shall no longer be a prey for the nations, nor shall beasts of the land devour them; but they shall dwell safely, and no one shall make them afraid. I will raise up for them a garden of renown, and they shall no longer be consumed with hunger in the land, nor bear the shame of the Gentiles anymore. Thus they shall know that I, the LORD their God, am with them, and they, the house of Israel, are My people," says the Lord GOD."'

"You are My flock, the flock of My pasture; you are men, and I am your God," says the Lord GOD.

Ezekiel 34, NKJV.

3

Tony Campolo

IT'S FRIDAY, BUT SUNDAY'S COMIN'

Tony Campolo is professor emeritus of sociology at Eastern University in St. Davids, Pennsylvania. He previously served for ten years on the faculty of the University of Pennsylvania. Founder of the Evangelical Association for the Promotion of Education (EAPE), Dr. Campolo has provided the leadership to create, nurture, and support programs for at-risk children in cities across the United States and Canada and has helped establish schools and universities in several developing countries.

He is well known for this sermon, which has been published in a book by the same title and released on video. This particular version was delivered October 9, 2001, in the chapel of North Park University in Chicago.

If there was ever a time that we could say, "These are the best of times and the worst of times," it would have to be right now. You're living in an incredible time, because it is the best of times and the worst of times.

The best of times because I can't remember a time when I have seen so much heroism. As those people were rushing down the steps to get out of the World Trade building, there were three hundred policemen and firemen running up the steps into the building to see if they could save lives. I don't know where that kind of courage comes from, but they did it and they lost their lives in the process. That is heroism that has to be respected.

My friend Gordon MacDonald spent a week at Ground Zero after the buildings collapsed, ministering to people. The stories he tells about the heroism, the self-sacrifice, and the ostracism that he saw. He said he's a Calvinist, but he has a hard time being a Calvinist because he is not convinced about the total depravity of human beings anymore. He saw so much goodness in that place.

The best of times, but also the worst of times. Profiling has reared its ugly head again. We're profiling people. And I have to tell you that this has dangerous implications, and we'd better be on guard against this because it seems like everyone is in favor of it now that we are in a time of an emergency. We're fighting against terrorists, but the truth of the matter is, Nietzsche had the answer when he said, "Beware, beware when you fight a dragon, lest you become a dragon." We have to be careful that in fighting those who would threaten liberties, we don't get rid of liberties; that in standing against those who would do away with freedom, we don't do away with freedom.

It's going to be a hard time for you as young people, figuring out how to balance things in the days that lie ahead, so that we're not foolish on the one hand, but the ugly face of racism doesn't rear itself in the disparaging ways that it has already reared itself in the last few weeks. We must not allow resentment to overtake us.

When Bill Clinton met Nelson Mandela for the first time, there was an incredible conversation. Bill Clinton asked Nelson Mandela, "When they released you from prison, I got Chelsea up at three in the morning because I wanted [to] have her see this. I knew it was a historic moment, and I got her out of bed to see you released from prison.

"As you walked across the courtyard, from the cell block to the gate of the prison, the television cameras focused in on your face. I have never seen such anger, such animosity, and such hatred. I mean, you usually can't see that so clearly revealed. It was all over you. It was intense hatred, intense resentment. President Mandela, that is not the Nelson Mandela that I know today. Could you explain what was going on?"

Nelson Mandela says, "You're the first one that brought that to my attention. I didn't know that anybody noticed that. But as they released me from the prison block and as I walked across the courtyard to the gate, I thought to myself, *They've taken everything away from me, my family is destroyed, my cause has been crushed, my friends are dead—anything, anybody, that meant anything to me, they've destroyed it all*, and I hated them with a fiery hatred. And then God spoke to me and said, 'Nelson, for twenty-seven years, you were their prisoner, but you were always a free man. Don't let them make you into a free man, only to turn you into their prisoner.'"

We have to be careful when we fight the dragon, lest we become the dragon. When it comes to profiling, I can only think of one friend of mine who talked about racism in a way that really made sense to me. As I got off the airplane at O'Hare, I thought of him because that is the last time I saw him. You may remember Peter Arnett from CNN. I ran into him one day in O'Hare, and I said, "Peter, I'm out of stories. Speakers live my stories. Do you have any good stories?"

He said, "I've got one for you. Last week I was on the West Bank, and a bomb went off, a terrorist bomb went off. Bodies were flying through the air. There was blood all over. A man came running up to me, holding in his hands a girl that was badly wounded, bloody from head to toe. The man holding this little girl in his arms said to me, 'Mister, the soldiers have sealed off the area. They won't let anybody in and anybody out. If I don't get her to a hospital, she is going to die. You can see that—that she is going to die if I don't get her out of here. You're the press; you can get us out of the lines. Please, please, will you help?'"

Peter told me, "What could I do? I put them in the back of the car, I covered them with a blanket, and we made our way through the lines. And on the way to Tel Aviv, he kept on saying, 'Go faster; please, mister, go faster.' And then he started moaning, 'I'm losing her, I'm losing her, I'm losing her!'"

Peter said, "When we got to the hospital, we rushed the girl into the operating room, dropped her on the table, came out, and sat on the bench outside the operating room totally dissipated and exhausted because of the tension that we had just been through. I was taking a deep breath when the doctor came out of the room and said, 'She's dead.' The man convulsed in tears. He screamed and he cried, and I put my arm around him and tried to comfort him. I said to him, 'I don't know what to say. I don't have any children. I don't know what it's like to lose a daughter.'

"The man looked up at me and said, 'Oh, that little girl isn't my daughter. That Palestinian girl is not my daughter. I am a Jewish settler.' And then he said, 'But maybe the time has come when all of us must learn to look on every child as a son and as a daughter. Maybe the day has come when we must discover what it means to be part of the family of God.'"

That day is here, and that day is now. We have to overcome the racism that is inherent in this present crisis. We must go beyond the resentment and the hatred that can easily be generated in such a setting. And we must learn from history. I don't know how many of you have friends and relatives who have gone out to the mission field to Muslim countries, but it's almost impossible to win converts away from the Muslim faith to the Christian faith, because the minute that we confront them with Christianity, immediately to the minds of Muslim people come the Crusades. You say, but that was a thousand years ago, I hardly know much about the Crusades—how many of them, where, who led them where. We don't know much about the Crusades, but there isn't a Muslim in the world that doesn't know about the Crusades. Where, in the name of Jesus, we slaughtered how many hundreds and thousands of innocent people, a lot of them women and children. And because we did not behave well at a particular juncture of human history, the cause of the gospel was set back immeasurably for a thousand years. We cannot let that happen again.

Osama bin Laden would love to turn this into a holy war of Christians against Muslims. We must not let that happen. We must do everything we can in these days to reach across the lines, to learn who Muslim people are, what they believe, what their convictions are. There must be a time of rapprochement.

I am an evangelical. I want to win every Muslim to Jesus Christ, but until they become my neighbors, until they know that I love them, I am not going to have a chance to do that. We cannot live out the Great Commission until we first live out the Great Commandment. We all want to go out and preach the gospel to all nations, but we don't want them to be our neighbors. They've got to be our neighbors before we can convince them about the Christ who dies for them.

Just remember what Martin E. Niemöller said at a time of conflict like this. He said, "What I must recognize is that my nation's enemies are not God's enemies, and even those that declare themselves as God's enemies are not God's enemies."

We have to affirm some things in this day and age. When you come to a mess like this, immediately people want to know the answer why. It was intriguing in the weeks following the tragedies in New York and in Washington how many ministers were on CNN, were on *Larry King Live*—and they were all asking the same question: "Why? How could this have happened? If God is all-powerful, if God is all-loving, how could this have happened?"

Now I know a lot of you are deeply in a reformed tradition and say, "Well, it is all part of God's plan." I am afraid that your mind and theology don't agree. I don't believe in a God who sends airplanes into buildings to teach a nation a lesson. That is not my God. I contend when those planes hit those buildings, God was the first one who cried, and that God's tears continue even with us till this day and time.

I don't think that we have taken evil seriously enough. We are inclined to say that God controls everything. There is an evil force in the universe. I don't know when it was, but the Scriptures let me know that there was a rebellion of Satan and Satan's cohorts. There was a rebellion against God before the foundation of the earth. Satan may be a lot of things, but Satan is not stupid. Satan would not have rebelled unless he believed that there was a good chance of winning. Satan would not have rebelled if he was not convinced that he could pull it off.

Zoroastrian people knew that there was a struggle throughout history between light and darkness, but they weren't sure who would win in the struggle, which side would triumph. They called upon people to join the side of light so that the balance of power would be on the side of righteousness. That was the essence of their religion.

In Judaism, there was the hope that God would triumph in history, that God would be victorious. The Hebrew prophets lived in the expectation that God would triumph in history. But it wasn't until Jesus came that we moved beyond hope to reassurance. When Jesus died on the cross, when He was resurrected from the grave, we then knew beyond a shadow of a doubt how the struggle between light and darkness, between good and evil, would turn out.

Satan knew that if ever there was a chance to destroy God, it was there on Calvary—God incarnated in a human being, God wrapped up in human weakness, says the Scripture, in the form of human weakness—now spread-eagle on a Roman cross. If ever God was vulnerable, it was in that hour. When He hung on the cross outside the city wall, God in the most vulnerable condition possible. And at the end of the day, Satan must have been dancing and singing, convinced that God had been defeated; that God was dead. Satan must have thought, *I am in charge of the universe now. My dominions will rule over the universe now.*

And then three days later, God staged a coup. Up from the grave He arose, with a mighty triumph over His foes. And from that day on, there would never be any doubt that Christ's victory would be a reality and that Jesus would win.

Oscar [Cullmann], one of the greatest theologians [born in Germany] to come out of Switzerland during World War II, wrote a book called *Christ [and] Time.* He wrote about two days in World War II that have crucial significance, D-day and V-day. He points out that in any war, there is a battle that determines the outcome of the war. In the Civil War, it was Gettysburg. In the Napoleonic Wars, it was Waterloo. After Waterloo, it was over. I mean, the war wasn't over, but it was over; everyone knew that Napoleon was defeated. After Gettysburg, it wasn't over, in the sense that they continued fighting, but there was no doubt as to how the war was going to end.

And on that day in June when the Allied forces landed on the beaches of Normandy, everyone on both sides knew that this was the day it would all be decided. They made a movie called *The Longest Day.* The Nazis knew that if they could drive the Allied forces back into the oceans, they would win the war. Contrarily, the Allies were convinced that if they could establish the beachhead, they would win the war. And at the end of the day, the good news was that the Allies had established a beachhead. It was at that point that Rommel, the head of the Nazi forces, secretly joined the plot to kill Hitler. The head of the Nazi army joined the plot to kill Hitler because he knew that Hitler would never ever give up, and he knew that the war was lost after the longest day. That day determined the end of the war.

But this should be noted, students, that between D-day and V-day, the day that the war actually ended, more people died; there was more suffering, more death, more devastation than at any other time. The point being what?

Oscar [Cullmann] said, "We live between God's D-day and God's V-day." On Calvary and with the Resurrection, the decisive battle was fought and won. Satan is defeated. Satan is a paper tiger now. There is no way he can win. He lost the decisive battle. If ever he had a chance, it was there and he blew it. And now we know how it will end. For those of you who are English majors, throw T. S. Eliot out the window. He didn't know what he was talking about. He sounds heavy, and every sophomore that is into existential angst loves to read T. S. Eliot. "This is the way the world will end"—you know the couplet—"Not with a bang, but a whimper."

No, that's not it, because with Calvary and the Resurrection, this is the way the world will end. The kingdoms of this world will become the kingdoms of our God, and He shall reign forever and ever and ever. Alleluia, alleluia. We live in that anticipation of victory. So when we see evil rear its ugly head, when we see the horrors of the World Trade buildings, we recognize the setback. We recognize the evil that was at work there. But we know that those evil forces have won a battle in a cause that they will ultimately lose.

And I am here to declare that it is better to lose a battle in a cause that ultimately wins than to win a battle in a cause that ultimately loses. Do you not agree? This is the good news of the gospel.

And in the context of all of this, we have to make sure that certain things are changed. If we are going to wipe out terrorism, it is not going to be because we are lobbing bombs or rockets into Afghanistan, and it will not even be because we send the troops in to weed out the terrorists in those caves. It will be because we changed the situation in the world today. You know very well that if we kill Bin Laden and every terrorist alive today, it will only be another couple of years before a new group of terrorists rise up to take their place because we have done nothing about the conditions that create terrorism.

This may seem unpopular in America, which is so pro-Israel, especially among evangelical Christians, who are more pro-Israel than most of the Jewish people in this country. You listen to evangelical fundamentalists on television, and they're all for the restoration of the state of Israel, who gets run over in the process. I find that my Jewish friends are much more sympathetic to the word *justice*. We have sat back and said absolutely nothing as Israeli tanks that we provided, guns that we have issued, have been used to level the houses of Palestinian people. We have gone into lands that belong to Palestinians. By law, by right, by UN declaration, that land belongs to the Palestinians. Israel had conceded that that land belongs to the Palestinians, and then after conceding that, they sent troops in, leveled the land, and built Jewish settlements there, and when boys and girls threw rocks at them, they couldn't quite figure out why and called these kids terrorists.

There is anger out there, and for all the evil of an Osama bin Laden, you've got to say this: "There will be no peace and justice and safety for Americans until there is peace and justice and safety for the Palestinian people."

Please, we must be committed to the preservation of the state of Israel, but we must be equally committed to justice for the Palestinians. May I point out now to you that the word *justice* appears in the Bible more often than the word *love*? That's because there is no love if there is no justice.

We have to understand Islam. I don't know much about Islam; do you? Do you really know that much about Islam, except that they pray five times a day and that they take this pilgrimage and walk around a black stone? I am not even sure what the stone represents. Do we understand why having a military base in Saudi Arabia is a sacrilege to Islamic people? We say we need to respect our Islamic brothers and sisters, but Saudi Arabia has been designated since the time of Mohammed as holy land on which infidels should not live. And when we establish a base there, it is [an] affront to everything they believe.

If we are going [to] respect other people's religions, then we have to pay the price for that. I know that base is important for keeping tabs on Iraq, but we've got to find another way of doing that without creating sacrilege. I am sure that most of us don't even know that we are creating sacrilege as a nation. We've got to understand these brothers and sisters.

We have to deal with the whole issue of poverty. You know that poverty is what breeds terrorism in the ultimate sense. I'm horrified, you're horrified, we're all horrified with this incredible tragedy, greater than Pearl Harbor. More than five thousand lost their lives in these acts of terrorism. We're shocked. We're depressed. We're in mourning. But let me remind you of something: while you were sleeping last night, thirty thousand children under the age of twelve died of either starvation or diseases related to malnutrition. Let me repeat that. Thirty thousand children under the age of twelve died of either starvation or diseases related to malnutrition, and we weren't shocked over that. We're not depressed over that. We're not crying over that. And it happens every day, every day, every day.

I contend that as Christian young people at a school that has a vision, your responsibility is to rise up and say, "I don't know what other schools are going to do with their students, but I am going to be a student from North Park University that is committed to the elimination of that world hunger." It can be done, you know. It has been projected by Christian Aid in London that we can cut the present level of poverty exactly in half in fifteen years.

We've already made tremendous progress. Twenty years ago, only two out of every five people had decent drinking water. Now it is four out of five. Twenty years ago, only four out of every ten children had a chance to go to school. Now it is seven out of every ten. We are making progress. The prophets of doom have conned us into thinking things are getting worse and worse and worse, but I am here to tell you that it is just not so. The same Jesus that rose again from the dead, that same Christ, is in us and working through us, driving back the forces of evil.

Let me just cite two things. Some years ago, a man by the name of Al Whittaker came down for breakfast. He was then the CEO of [Bristol-]Myers Corporation, a large multinational corporation. Receiving breakfast, his wife looks across the table and says, "Al, is this what you want to do the rest of your life? Do you want to spend the rest of your life making rich people richer? Because that is what you are doing. You are making us rich. You're making the stockholders rich. But I am not sure that producing men's cologne is a great contribution to humanity."

He thought about that all day long. That night over supper, he said to his wife, "The question you asked troubled me. So much so that you should know that as I left the office today, I handed in my resignation." He started an organization known as Opportunities International. This was an attempt to get at people like you to get the vision to go into third-world countries, among the poor and the oppressed, and start small business[es] and cottage industries that the people can own and run themselves.

I remember starting the first of those, the very first. It was in the Dominican Republic. It was part of your missionary enterprise that we got connected with them. We started a little factory in a slum area called Guachapeta. Twenty women got together and started this little factory. They were making sandals out of old automobile tires. They told the boys and girls in the village, "Every time you bring us a discarded, worn-out automobile tire, we'll give you fifty cents." It wasn't long before they had every old automobile tire in Santo Domingo. Then they started getting a lot of new automobile tires. And they began to realize that God works in wondrous ways.

In Philadelphia, we started a wonderful little company where we got the telephone company to give us their old telephones. Nobody fixes things anymore; they just throw them away. Something breaks, and the cost of labor is so high that they don't fix them. So the telephone company ended up with thousands of telephones that were broken but not useless. They gave them to us with great appreciation, because they got a tax write-off for thousands of phones given to a charity.

And you say, "I know what you're thinking, Campolo. You got those kids to fix those phones. We're not that smart; we don't know how to fix things." But if you're from the city like I am, you are good at one thing: taking things apart. Oh, how we know how to do that. We took the phones apart, tested the parts, and when we found working parts, we packaged them, wrapped them up, and we sold the parts to phone companies. It was a good deal. The business doesn't exist anymore because they were subject to a buyout by the phone company, who bought them out for a quarter of a million dollars, which wasn't bad for a group of ten guys who had previously been on the corner selling drugs and who knows what else. A quarter of a million dollars was divided up between them, but more than that, they were given a deal where they ended up working for the phone company doing the same thing at $17 an hour.

You've got to attack poverty. Poverty breeds terrorism. Injustice breeds terrorism. We've got to address those issues as Christians. We must work for justice. We must work to end poverty. I can't say it strongly enough.

In the midst of all that's going on right now, let me give you the really hard thing to swallow. Of all the things I should not mention today in this chapel, I shouldn't mention Jesus. Now that's a shocker.

The last thing we want to hear right now in the midst of your present conflicts is Jesus. When down deep inside, we all know what Jesus said. And the question that I have is, "Do you hold on to Jesus when it is not a problem? Is that when you hold on to Jesus, when it is not a problem?"

I want to tell you it is a problem to hold on to Jesus right now. I am pleased that the president of the United States decided to drop food in addition to bombs, but I have got to tell you this. It is about time we take seriously what the Scriptures say. If your enemy hungers, feed him. If your enemy is naked, clothe him. You return good for evil.

Does Jesus mean this for all places, all times, all peoples, all circumstances, or just when it is convenient? What does it really mean to follow the one who said, "Blessed are the peacemakers: for they shall be called the children of God"? We all want to be children of God, but we don't like the conditions. What do you do with a Senator McCain who says, "I hope God shows them some mercy, because they're not going to get any from us"?

I've got news for you. The beatitudes say that if you refuse to be merciful, then don't expect to receive mercy. Blessed are the merciful, for they are the ones who will receive mercy. I thought that the best prayer I heard in the midst of the praying that has gone on this month came at that wonderful prayer meeting in the Capitol Dome as the senator for Maryland stood. When Ms. [Mikulski] got to the microphone, she prayed, "Dear God, bring those who have committed these horrible deeds to . . . ," and I am waiting for her to say "justice" because that is what America was talking about, but she prayed, ". . . to repentance."

There is the Christian prayer. I don't wish the destruction of my enemies; I wish my enemies to repent, even as I need to repent. There needs to be repentance on both sides of the line. After all, we need to do some repenting, do we not? We're 7 percent of the world's population, and we consume 43 percent of the world's resources. We have lived lives of affluence. Everybody loves to talk about the sins of Sodom and Gomorrah. I've heard these evangelists say, "The reason why this is happening is because we are committing the sins of Sodom and Gomorrah!" You've heard that line, haven't you?

It is about time you read the Bible. If you go to Ezekiel 16:49, these are the words you will read: "This was the iniquity of your sister Sodom: She and her daughter had pride, fullness of food, and abundance of idleness; neither did she strengthen the hand of the poor and the needy." Read the Bible. The thing that is wrong with most fundamentalists is they are so busy arguing the infallibility of Scripture that they never even bother to read it.

The truth of the matter is this: the sin of Sodom and the sin of Gomorra[h] were much more than sexual improprieties, which they were, but much more than just that. We get fixated on that. You know if we don't commit fornication or adultery or any of the other sexual sins, then we somehow think that we're pure, that we're holy, and the Bible is clear on this one.

To care about the poor and the oppressed is at the core of the Christian gospel. May I say, there are more than two thousand verses of Scripture that call upon us to minister to the poor and the oppressed. No other Scripture passages can measure up to the passages on poverty. And this is our calling.

I have to ask you as students what you are going to do, because our task is not to get people saved into heaven when they die. I am glad that I am a Christian, because when I do die, I will be with Christ. The older I get, the more comforting that is. I am getting old. My idea of a happy hour is a nap. I am over the hill, so that part of the message of the gospel is of crucial significance for me.

But you're young. I remember when I was a kid. When I was twelve years old, I was sitting in church and my pastor said, "Are you ready to die?" I'm twelve years old. I can still hear him say, "You don't think you're going to die, but you could leave this church and walk across the street and get hit by a truck. Then where would you be?" That didn't get me saved; it made me very careful about crossing the streets.

And then there was always threat number two, left behind. In our day, it was another movie, *Thief in the Night*. You don't have to die; the trumpet could sound and the Lord returns. That was used in everything. "Pastor, is it all right to go to movies?" "What if you are in the movies and the trumpet sounds and the Lord returns?" The next time I went to the movies, I was scared to death. I was sure I was going to get halfway through the flick and the trumpet would sound, and I could just see myself going through eternity, shaking people, saying, "How did it end? How did that movie end?"

I believe in the Second Coming. I don't know when it is going to happen. I don't feel bad about that. Jesus didn't know when it was going to happen. They asked Him, "When will You return and set up Your kingdom?" He said, "I don't know when. You're going to have to ask an American evangelist for the answer to that one."

I have news for you. I believe in the Second Coming for a very important reason: the God who is at work in us and through us is coming back, and what we do not complete, which is most of it, and what we do not achieve, he will come and join up with us and carry us to victory. Once again, Oscar [Cullmann] said, "If you had talked to the French Underground during World War II and asked them what they were doing, they'd say, 'We're overthrowing the Nazi army.' They'd say, 'You're a ragtime army with a few grenades and a few rifles. You're going to take on the huge Nazi military machine and beat them?' The answer would have been, 'You don't understand. Across the English Channel, there is a huge invasion force assembling, even as we speak. We don't know when the signal will be given, but one of these days, that huge invasion force will sweep across the English Channel, join up with us, and carry us to victory.'"

That's my message. As we struggle against the forces of darkness, as we work to overcome poverty, as we bring justice as best we know how into the world, people will laugh at us and say, "You can't possibly win. You're too weak; your forces are too feeble." But I am here to declare the good news. Beyond the skies, there is a huge invasion force being assembled, and I don't know when they are going to sound that trumpet, but one of these days, that invasion force is going to come into our historical situation and join up with us and carry us to victory. That is why we do not labor as those without hope.

That's why I call upon you as students. Listen, I beg of you, don't waste your lives. Lay them on the line for the work of the kingdom. You say, "What do you want, everyone to become a missionary?" Yes. What is there that's interesting to do anyway? Going to work for American Airlines, you'll be out of a job next week.

People, there is so much to be done. And you know and I know that you have dreams and visions of doing good. You have had them, haven't you? I don't know where it hits you. At a Baptist revival during the fiftieth verse of "Just as I Am" or at a Presbyterian revival during the fiftieth verse of "Kumbaya." I don't know. But somewhere, someplace— be honest—God spoke to you, and you had a sense that you could do something splendid, something miraculous, something incredible with your life.

In 1987, I spoke at the Urbana Conference, and Billy Graham stepped aside and let me be the one that gave the invitation for missionary service. They only do it once in that weekend, and he said, "I want you to do it." It was an incredible response—thousands and thousands of young people committing themselves to missionary service.

Afterward, Billy Graham said, "That was wonderful. I bet we come away with at least a couple of hundred missionaries out of this meeting."

I said, "There were thousands."

He said, "Yes, there were thousands, but they'll go home and they'll be talked out of it. And you know who will talk them out of it— their parents."

Jesus wasn't kidding when He said, "When you get a vision of doing incredible things for God, the first opponents will be those in your own household. Think not that I have come to bring peace." We listen to *Focus on the Family* and think, "If you just become Christians, it's all going to become well in the family." Jesus says it's not that way. When you become Christians, mothers will be set against daughters, daughters against mothers, fathers against sons, sons against fathers. When you stand up and say, "Mom, my life belongs to Jesus," like St. Francis, your own mother will probably turn upon you and say, "Look, I didn't send you to school to go traipsing off to some place and accomplish nothing. There is a lot that you can do right here at home."

You've heard it, haven't you? I know what your parents tell you, and they're wrong. They said, "Go to a university. Go to North Park. It's a good university and you will get a good education, and if you get a good education, then you will get a good job, and if you get a good job, you will make a lot of money, and if you make a lot of money, you will be able to buy a lot of stuff."

That's what it's about, people: stuff. The sizes of American houses have increased 20 percent in floor space in just ten years. Why? Because we have more and more children, bigger and bigger families? Is that why we are building bigger houses? No, we need bigger houses just to hold all the stuff. When it's Christmas, your parents have to go up to your rooms and shovel half the stuff out to make room for all the new stuff. That's what it's about.

Many of you aren't here for an education. You just want that credential that will enable you to get the position that will get you the money to get the stuff. How many of you could pass your exams from two years ago? Let me ask you the next question: What did you do with your textbooks? Sold them. You forgot what you learned, you sold the textbooks, and you call this higher education.

You need to get some perspective on things. God has called every one of you here to lay your lives on the line and become "living sacrifices," which is the only reasonable thing to do with your life. I don't know how you are going to invest your life. You've got to take a good look at your talents and the opportunities available to you. But I call upon you to optimize your life for Jesus Christ.

You've got to ask yourself, "In what way can I contribute to changing the world into the kind of world that God wants it to be?" We are called upon to be world changers for the kingdom. And when we pray the Lord's Prayer, we pray, "Thy kingdom come, Thy will be done." Where? "On earth."

I don't know what this war is going to accomplish, to tell the truth, because my Bible says that those who live by the sword die by the sword. We don't want to believe that right now. We want to believe those who live by the sword triumph and live happily ever after. Jesus didn't know what He was talking about.

We have got to face up to what we call real politics, and I contend that Jesus was the only real politician that ever lived. He understood what it was all about. I contend that as a Christian college, we look beyond the existential situation and ask, "What can we do to alter the course of history?"

I brought along some friends today. They started a program called Mission Year. They call upon young people to take a year off from school, perhaps between college and graduate school, perhaps taking off a year just to get some perspective. Ideally, I think it is great between sophomore and junior years to take a year off. What we do is put these young people together in small groups, six to a group, five groups to a city, thirty young people there in the city. There are about twenty-five of these young people starting up a program in Chicago. They rent a house. They live together in community. They connect with the church, but they don't exercise leadership in the church. They sing in the choir maybe, or they go to the services, but they don't exercise leadership because they're going to be gone at the end of the year. They spend about fifteen or twenty hours a week at soup kitchens, AIDS hospices, old folks homes, tutoring, going into schools and saying to the principal, "I have fifteen hours a week. I can come in here and help any teacher you want during the school day."

They impact the community with a presence. Then they spend twenty hours a week getting to know people in the neighborhood. Knocking on doors, saying, "Hey, we're here in the neighborhood. Don't get nervous; I am not trying to a lay a trip on you or convert you. I just want to pray with you. Will you let us pray with you? Pray God's blessing on you."

Whether the people are Jewish or agnostic or Islamic, it doesn't make any difference. Nobody says no to a prayer. Usually you'll get, "If it makes you feel any better, go ahead."

"We don't have to come in. We can do it right here on the doorstep."

Then we ask the next question: "Do you have any special needs? Anything we should hold before God as we pray?" It is amazing what people will say. "My husband's lost his job. Will you pray he gets another one?" "My son's on drugs. He gets worse every month. Could you pray for him?" "I've got a daughter who is pregnant for the second time, and we don't know what to do with the first one." And then we pray.

You say, "That's it? You pray?" When we all get back to the house, we go over the cards of the people we visited. "Here's a guy that needs a job. The YMCA runs a job placement service. Let's call them and tell them to do something, to send someone over to that house. This girl is pregnant. The Catholics run the crisis pregnancy center. Let's tell them about this girl and have them send someone over to visit. That boy that's on drugs, let's call Team Challenge." We find that if you work in the city, you don't have to invent new programs. The programs are already there. The problem is that the people who desperately need the programs don't go.

You know seminaries, without exception, have a "Field of Dreams" mentality. Remember the movie *Field of Dreams*? "Build it, and they will come." Build the building and the program, and they will come. And that is all they do—tell us how to design programs. They never tell us how to market.

In reality, you've got to go out there and connect people with the ministries, and that's what we do. You see, you can't fail, because you can never say the program didn't work out well. It's not your program. And it is a win-win situation. White kids get along great in black neighborhoods, as long as they don't come in to compete with the programs that already exist. As long as you are there to feed people into the programs that the indigenous people have already created.

Praying with people. I got off the Bart Transportation system in Oakland, trying to find the teams that are in Oakland. There are six of them in Oakland, and I wanted to meet with them. They were all getting together at this Methodist church, and I couldn't find the church. I asked these two ladies, "Can you tell me where the Methodist church is?"

One of the ladies said, "Yeah, just up the street there." The other one said, "No, no, no. He's talking about that other church around the corner." Then she added, "He's talking about that church where they pray for everybody."

What an interesting concept, a church that prays for everybody. I have heard them say about a church, "They have great preaching." I've heard them say about a church, "They have a great youth program or a great social action program or a great music program." You've heard all those things about churches. When was the last time you heard them say, "There's a church that prays for everybody in the neighborhood"? Maybe it's time to clear out a lot of the stuff and make room for a house of prayer.

Maybe it's time to get into that kind of ministry, so I am inviting you, I am begging you as best as I know how, that you take seriously giving a year of your life to mission. If, after all, Mormon kids will give two years of their lives, I want to know why North Park kids won't give one year. Maybe the Mormons know what commitment is all about and we don't, even though we talk about it all the time. Could you give a year?

You say, "But I am going to medical school." You'll be a different kind of doctor. You say, "But I am going to law school." You'll be a different kind of lawyer. "I am going to be a teacher." You'll be a different kind of teacher. You need what they can do for you. Why do you think Jesus said to the rich young rulers, "Sell everything you have and give to the poor"? Because He wanted to eliminate poverty, which, of course, He does?

That isn't why He said to the rich young ruler, "Sell everything you have and give it to the poor." He said it to the rich young ruler because He knew what would happen to the rich young ruler when he went among the poor. He knew that in that world, the rich young ruler would be transformed and become a true disciple.

Whenever we send people into the inner city, they always say, "Is it safe?" They probably said that to you when you told them you were coming to North Park University. "Is it safe?"

And I always ask the same question: "Is it safe to live in that affluent suburban neighborhood? To live out your life in shopping centers? Is that safe?" Because my Bible says this: "More dangerous than those who destroy the body are those who destroy the soul." And I am looking at a generation of young people whose souls have been eaten up by an affluent, spoiled way of life. You need to get to the poor people so that your head can be put together again.

The best way to end this thing, in this day of dismal despair, is to end with my favorite story. It is tough to be a preacher who's made his whole living on one story. Even people that don't like me say, "He's got one good story. And we'll have him speak if he tells that one story, because we don't like anything else he says."

I belong to a black church. I didn't join one. It was a white church, and black people moved in and the white people left, and we didn't move. We're Italian; we don't move. The church became all black, and it's a great church. I am the last white. I would have done much better today if I had had my congregation here, because white people (and most of you are white) are hard to talk to. Black people are easy. Even when you are not doing well in the black church, they'll let you know.

One time I was halfway through a sermon and some lady in the back yelled, "Help him, Jesus; help him, Jesus." I knew it wasn't going well. Likewise, in my church, when you are pumping all cylinders, my deacons would be right here with me, right up front, and anytime I said something good, they say, "Preach, preach man, preach." That's what I needed today; I needed my deacons.

The women in my church, when you are pumping all cylinders, they don't say, "Amen," or "Hallelujah." That's white. They do this, one hand in the air. You say something good, they'll say, "Well"—that's it. That doesn't sound like much. You get fifty, sixty women saying, "Well," and your hormones bubble. And the men in my church, when you are delivering the gospel, they're up on their feet, yelling, "Keep going, man; keep going." I don't get that from white North Park students. I don't get "Keep going"; I get "Stop."

Once a year, we have a preach-off in our church. You don't even know what they are, do you? You get five to seven preachers back to back to see who's best. You never say that. You say it's for the glory of God.

It was my turn to preach, and I do not want to brag, but I was good. I knew I was good, because the deacons were yelling, "Preach," and the women were saying, "Well," and the men were going, "Keep going," and I feed on that stuff. The more they did it, the better I got. The better I got, the more they did it. I got so good, I wanted to take notes on me.

When I ended, that place exploded. There was shouting; there was screaming. It was incredible. It was just ballistic. I sat down, and I said, "Pastor, you're next. You going to be able to top that?"

He said, "Son, sit back, because your old man is going to do you in." I was so hot that day, I didn't think anyone could do me in, and he did me in. One line. "Friday, but Sunday's comin'."

That's it, one line. Didn't sound like much, but you weren't there. It was Friday, and He was spiked to that Roman cross, and He was dead, but that was Friday. Sunday's comin'. Somebody yelled, "Keep going, keep going." And that's all he needed. He took off. "Friday, Friday people are saying, 'As things have been, so they shall be. You can't change anything in this world.' But they didn't know it was only Friday. Sunday's comin'."

Now I thought I would get something from this crowd by now. We have to "de-honky-tize" this crowd. I will give you one more chance.

It's Friday, and they're saying, "A bunch of students in a small Christian college at the edge of Chicago—they cannot alter history; they cannot end poverty; they cannot stand against injustice and win." But they don't know it's only Friday. Sunday's comin'.

I can still remember the end of that sermon. He just yelled at the top of his lungs, "Friday." Without hesitation, the crowd yelled back, "Sunday's comin'."

That's the good news. When we hear the gospel and respond to it, not just with our heads and our hearts, but with our will, with our lives, when we give ourselves to the kingdom of God on earth to create the kind of world that God wants it to be, we've got the good news. And the good news is this: It's Friday, but Sunday's comin'.

Used by permission of Tony Campolo.

4

Aimee Semple McPherson

BEHOLD THE MAN!

———

Then came Jesus out, wearing the crown of thorns and the purple robe. And Pilate said to them, "Behold the Man!"
—*John 19:5* NKJV

Jesus has promised us in His Word that He, if HE is lifted up from the earth, will draw all men unto Himself, and before beginning this subject today, I cried out to the Lord to help me to sink out of sight and to lift Him up above the earth until you should see no man save Jesus only.

BEHOLD the Man! Behold THE Man! Behold the MAN! I would like to repeat it over and over again until I catch every wandering mind and bring each straying thought into captivity. Behold the Man. Just close your eyes to all else for a few moments.

STOP beholding your business—your pleasure—your home—your earthly cares and duties—your neighbor—whatever it may be that has been absorbing your attention, and *behold the Man, Christ Jesus*.

If you have never stopped long enough before in your busy life to behold the Man, the Lamb of God, the One who loves you more than any earthly friend loves you, I want you to behold Him NOW.

I am sure that if you could only get one glimpse of that face which is the fairest among ten thousand; if you could only catch one cadence of His voice, sweet as the rushing of many waters; if you could only gaze for one moment into the depths of those tender eyes filled with understanding and sympathy and love, the tears of love and gratitude would spring to your eyes, your heart would fill with praise till you would never wish to cease from beholding and adoring and worshiping this Man, Christ Jesus. As the shades of darkness and unbelief are driven back by the light of the sun of righteousness, and as you behold the Man, you will find new beauties, new attributes and graces unfolding themselves before your astonished and adoring eyes each moment you behold, till your heart bursts forth into singing,

> Since mine eyes were fixed on Jesus,
> I've lost sight of all beside,
> So enhanced my Spirit's vision,
> Gazing at the crucified.

As we sweep back the curtains of the centuries and look back through the undimmed corridors of the past, we behold the Man seated with His Father upon His throne. He was with His Father from the beginning—the brightest jewel in heaven, the joy of the Father, the delight of the angels, the light of the temple, the only begotten Son, worthy of praise upon harps of gold, and the angels fell prostrate at His feet as He sat in His kingly robes and splendor in their midst.

Behold the Man filled with sorrow on that memorable day when our ancestral parents fell into sin and because of that sin were banished from the sight of God under penalty of death. And when there was no eye to pity, no arm to save, none that could pay the ransom price for their redemption, we:

Behold the Man saying: "Father, send me; I will pay the price. Without the shedding of blood there is no remission of sins; I will shed my blood, Father; I will be the bridge to span the gulf 'twixt man and God." Then we read that "God so loved the world, that he gave his only begotten Son, that whosoever believeth in him should not perish, but have everlasting life" [John 3:16 KJV].

Behold the Man standing up to take leave of the Father, leaving the songs and the adoration of the angelic hosts, laying aside His royal robes, His scepter, and His crown, stepping down from the throne and coming all the way from heaven to earth for you and me, that we might not perish but have everlasting life.

Behold the Man living and growing up with Mary, His mother, and Joseph, in the carpenter shop. Behold Him at the age of thirty, baptized of John in the river Jordan, ready to begin His ministry. Behold the Man rising from a watery grave as the heavens opened and the Holy Sprit descended upon Him and the voice of God spoke aloud, saying, "This is My beloved Son, in whom I am well pleased." Thus He entered upon His ministry with divine authority and the power of the Godhead resting upon Him and abiding with Him.

Behold the Man tempted in the wilderness for forty days, tempted in all points like as we, and yet without sin. Behold Him turning the water into wine, preaching the gospel of the kingdom, healing the sick, cleansing the leper, raising the dead, opening the eyes of the blind, unstopping the deaf ears, feeding the hungry multitudes, calming the troubled sea, weeping over Jerusalem, forgiving the sinner, giving water to the thirsty, healing the brokenhearted.

Behold the Man—the King of glory—walking in humility upon this earth, footsore and weary. Behold Him praying alone, night after night on the mountainside, praying for you, dear heart, and for a sleeping world who would never appreciate nor understand. The birds had their nests, the foxes their holes, but the Son of Man had nowhere to lay His head.

Behold the Man at the Last Supper, when even though His heart was aching, even though He knew the hand that would betray Him, and the disciple that would deny Him, even though He knew that all would forsake Him and flee away, His thoughts were for you and for me when He vowed that He would drink no more of the fruit of the vine until He drank it anew with us in His Father's kingdom, saying: "As oft as ye do this, ye do show forth My death till I come." Oh, glorious bridge that spans the long, silent years from the day of His death till the day He shall come.

Behold the Man praying in the garden alone while His disciples slumbered and slept. Behold His agony and the travail of His soul as He cried: "Nevertheless not my will, but thine, be done . . . And being in an agony he prayed more earnestly: and his sweat was as it were great drops of blood falling down to the ground" [Luke 22:42, 44 KJV]

Behold the Man bending low over His disciples in His sorrow, craving one understanding heart to watch with Him. But He found them sleeping and said unto them: "Why sleep ye? rise and pray. . . . And while he yet spake, behold a multitude," pressing on through the gray dawn of morning, coming with staves and swords to take this Man—this Jesus of yours, and mine [Luke 22:46–47 KJV].

Behold the Man led as a sheep to the slaughter, and as a lamb before his shearers is dumb, so He opened not His mouth. Behold Him despised and rejected of men, a Man of sorrows and acquainted with grief. Behold Him bearing our griefs, carrying our sorrows, wounded for our transgressions, bruised for our iniquities. He was taken from prison and from judgment.

Behold the Man condemned to die by the multitude He loved and longed to gather in His arms. Behold Him beaten with stripes and nailed to the cross. The crown of thorns was placed upon His brow; the Roman spear pierced His side. But, oh, beloved, hear Him cry, "Father, forgive them, they know not what they do!" Then when the debt had been paid, when He had borne our penalty (death) in His own body on the tree, hear the glad triumphant words that rang through the sky that hour, and still resound through the earth today:

"IT IS FINISHED." Then behold the Man as midst rending rocks and darkening sky, He bowed His head and gave up the ghost.

Behold the Man lying wrapped in the cold silence of death in the tomb. Then in the early dawn of the third day, as the first gold and purple rays of morning rose in glad triumph above the hills of Jerusalem, an angel from heaven spread his great white pinions and, sweeping down from heaven to earth, rolled the great stone away from the mouth of the sepulcher.

Behold the Man resurrected, rising and coming forth again to look upon the world—His world, purchased by His blood. Behold Him again, living and loving, walking and talking with His people, feeding the hungry, encouraging the downcast.

Behold the Man leading captivity captive, ascending on high to give gifts unto men, saying: "It is expedient for you that I go away, for if I go not away from you, the Comforter will not come. But if I go away, I will not leave you comfortless; I will send another, even the Holy Ghost. If I go away, I will come again and take you unto Myself, that where I am there ye may be also," and the clouds received Him out of their sight.

Behold the Man seated again at the right hand of God the Father. Behold Him standing at your side just now as revealed by the Spirit; hear Him say: "Behold, I stand at the door and knock. If any man will open to Me, I will come in and sup with him and he with Me." Let Him in, dear heart; draw nigh to Him, and He will draw nigh to you. Receive the Holy Spirit which He has sent to lead you into all truth. Be faithful a little longer. Then soon, yea, very soon, you will

BEHOLD THE MAN coming in the clouds of heaven with power and great glory to take you to Himself, where in the midst of joys unbounded as the waves of the ocean, we will behold the Man by the glassy sea, and worship in adoration at His throne, our Redeemer, our Bridegroom forevermore. Open your eyes just now, dear heart. Oh!

BEHOLD THE MAN!

5

Martin Luther

SERMON FOR THE FOURTH SUNDAY AFTER EPIPHANY (ROMANS 13:8–10)

———

Martin Luther (1483–1546) was the infamous reformer who nailed his Ninety-five Theses to the Wittenberg church door on October 31, 1517, exposing the abuses of the papacy. The heart of Luther's message was justification by faith. The following is taken from his Church Postil.

CHRISTIAN LOVE AND THE COMMAND TO LOVE

1. This, like the two preceding epistle lessons, is admonitory, and directs our attention to the fruits of faith. Here, however, Paul sums up briefly all the fruits of faith, in love. In the verses going before, he enjoined subjection to temporal government—the rendering of tribute, custom, fear, and honor wherever due—since all governmental power is ordained of God. Then follows our lesson: "Owe no man anything," etc.

2. I shall ignore the various explanations usually invented for this command, "Owe no man anything, but to love one another." To me,

clearly and simply it means: Not as men, but as Christians, are we under obligations. Our indebtedness should be the free obligation of love. It should not be compulsory and law-prescribed. Paul holds up two forms of obligation: one is inspired by law, the other by love.

Legal obligations make us debtors to men; an instance is when one individual has a claim upon another for debt. The duties and tribute, the obedience and honor, we owe to political government are of this legal character. Though personally these things are not essential to the Christian—they do not justify him nor make him more righteous—yet, because he must live here on earth, he is under obligation, so far as outward conduct is concerned, to put himself on a level with other men in these things, and generally to help maintain temporal order and peace. Christ paid tribute money as a debt (Matthew 17:27), notwithstanding He had told Peter He was under no obligation to do so and would have committed no sin before God in omitting the act.

3. Another obligation is love, when a Christian voluntarily makes himself a servant of all men. Paul says (1 Corinthians 9:19), "For though I was free from all men, I brought myself under bondage to all." This is not a requirement of human laws; no one who fails in this duty is censured or punished for neglect of legal obligations. The world is not aware of the commandment to love; of the obligation to submit to and serve a fellow man. This fact is very apparent. Let one have wealth, and so long as he refrains from disgracing his neighbor's wife, from appropriating his neighbor's goods, sullying his honor, or injuring his person, he is, in the eyes of the law, righteous. No law punishes him for avarice and penuriousness; for refusing to lend, to give, to aid, and to help his wronged neighbor secure justice. Laws made for restraint of the outward man are directed only toward evil works, which they prohibit and punish. Good works are left to voluntary performance. Civil law does not extort them by threats and punishment, but commends and rewards them, as does the Law of Moses.

4. Paul would teach Christians to so conduct themselves toward men and civil authority as to give no occasion for complaint or censure because of unfulfilled indebtedness to temporal law. He would not have them fail to satisfy the claims of legal obligation, but rather to go beyond its requirements, making themselves debtors voluntarily and serving those who have no claims on them. Relative to this topic, Paul says (Romans 1:14), "I am debtor both to Greeks and to Barbarians." Love's obligation enables a man to do more than is actually required of him. Hence the Christian always willingly renders to the state and to the individual all service exacted by temporal regulations, permitting no claims upon himself in this respect.

5. Paul's injunction, then, might be expressed: Owe all men, that you may owe none; owe everything, that you may owe nothing. This sounds paradoxical. But one indebtedness is that of love, an obligation to God. The other is indebtedness to temporal law, an obligation in the eyes of the world. He who makes himself a servant, who takes upon himself love's obligation to all men, goes so far that no one dares complain of omission; indeed, he goes farther than any could desire. Thus he is made free. He lives under obligation to no one from the very fact that he puts himself under obligation to all. This manner of presenting the thought would be sustained by the Spirit in connection with other duties; for instance: Do no good work, that you may do only good works. Never be pious and holy, if you would be always pious and holy. As Paul says (Romans 12:16), "Be not wise in your own conceits"; or (1 Corinthians 3:18) "If any man thinketh that he is wise among you in this world, let him become a fool, that he may become wise." It is in this sense we say: Owe all men, that you may owe no man; or "Owe no man anything, but to love one another."

6. Such counsel is given with the thought of the two obligations. He who would perform works truly good in the sight of God must guard against works seemingly brilliant in the eyes of the world, works

whereby men presume to become righteous. He who desires to be righteous and holy must guard against the holiness attained by works without faith. Again, the seeker for wisdom must reject the wisdom of men, of nature, wisdom independent of the Spirit. Similarly, he who would be under obligation to none must obligate himself to all in every respect. So doing, he retains no claim of his own. Consequently, he soon rises superior to all law, for law binds only those who have claims of their own. Rightly is it said, "Qui cedit omnibus bonis, omnibus satisfecit," "He who surrenders all his property satisfies all men." How can one be under obligation when he does not, and cannot, possess anything? It is love's way to give all. The best way, then, to be under obligation to none is through love to obligate one's self in every respect to all men. In this sense it may be said: If you would live, die; if you would not be imprisoned, incarcerate yourself; if you do not desire to go to hell, descend there; if you object to being a sinner, be a sinner; if you would escape the cross, take it upon yourself; if you would conquer the devil, let him vanquish you; would you overcome a wicked individual, permit him to overcome you. The meaning of it all is we should readily submit to God, to the devil, and to men, and willingly permit their pleasure; we are to insist on nothing, but to accept all things as they transpire. This is why Paul speaks as he does, "Owe no man anything," etc., instead of letting it go at the preceding injunction in verse 5, "Render therefore to all their dues," etc.

LOVE FULFILLS THE LAW

For he that loveth his neighbor hath fulfilled the law.

7. Having frequently spoken of the character and fruits of love, it is unnecessary to introduce the subject here. The topic is sufficiently

treated in the epistle lesson for the Sunday preceding Lent. We will look at the command to love in the Law of God. Innumerable, endless, are the books and doctrines produced for the direction of man's conduct. And there is still no limit to the making of books and laws. Note the ecclesiastical and civil regulations, the spiritual orders and stations. These laws and doctrines might be tolerated, might be received with more favor, if they were founded upon and administered according to the one great law—the one rule or measure—of love; as the Scriptures do, which present many different laws, but all born of love, and comprehended in and subject to it. And these laws must yield, must become invalid, when they conflict with love.

Of Love's higher authority we find many illustrations in the Scriptures. Christ makes particular mention of the matter in Matthew 12:3–4, where David and his companions ate the holy showbread. Though a certain law prohibited all but the priests from partaking of this holy food, Love was empress here, and free. Love was over the Law, subjecting it to herself. The Law had to yield for the time being, had to become invalid, when David suffered hunger. The Law had to submit to the sentence: "David hungers and must be relieved, for Love commands, Do good to your needy neighbor. Yield, therefore, thou Law. Prevent not the accomplishment of this good. Rather accomplish it thyself. Serve him in his need. Interpose not thy prohibitions." In connection with this same incident, Christ teaches that we are to do good to our neighbor on the Sabbath; to minister as necessity demands, whatever the Sabbath restrictions of the Law. For when a brother's need calls, Love is authority and the Law of the Sabbath is void.

8. Were laws conceived and administered in love, the number of laws would matter little. Though one might not hear or learn all of them, he would learn from the one or two he had knowledge of, the principle of love taught in all. And though he were to know all laws, he might not discover the principle of love any more readily than he

would in one. Paul teaches this method of understanding and mastering law when he says: "Owe no man anything, but to love one another"; "He that loveth another hath fulfilled the law"; "If there be any other commandment, it is briefly comprehended in this saying, namely, Thou shalt love thy neighbor as thyself"; "Love worketh no ill to his neighbor"; "Love is the fulfilling of the law." Every word in this epistle lesson proves Love mistress of all law.

9. Further, no greater calamity, wrong, and wretchedness is possible on earth than the teaching and enforcing of laws without love. In such case, laws are but a ruinous curse, making true the proverb, "Summum jus, summa injustitia," "The most strenuous right is the most strenuous wrong"; and again, Solomon's words (Ecclesiastes 7:17), "Noli nimium esse justus," "Be not righteous overmuch." Here is where we leave unperceived the beam in our own eye and proceed to remove the mote from our neighbor's eye. Laws without love make the conscience timid and fill it with unreasonable terror and despair, to the great injury of body and soul. Thus much trouble and labor are incurred, all to no purpose.

10. An illustration in point is the before-mentioned incident of David in his hunger (1 Samuel 21:6). Had the priest been disposed to refuse David the holy bread, had he blindly insisted on honoring the prohibitions of the Law and failed to perceive the authority of Love, had he denied this food to him who hungered, what would have been the result? So far as the priest's assistance went, David would have had to perish with hunger, and the priest would have been guilty of murder for the sake of the Law. Here, indeed, "summum jus, summa injustitia"—the most strenuous right would have been the most strenuous wrong. Moreover, on examining the heart of the priest who should be so foolish, you would find there the extreme abomination of making sin where there is no sin, and a matter of conscience where there is no occasion for it. For he holds it a sin to eat the bread, when

really it is an act of love and righteousness. Then, too, he regards his act of murder—permitting David to die of hunger—not a sin, but a good work and service to God.

11. But who can fully portray this blind, perverted, abominable folly? It is the perpetration of an evil the devil himself cannot outdo. For it makes sin where there is no sin, and a matter of conscience without occasion. It robs of grace, salvation, virtue, and God with all His blessings, and that without reason, falsely and deceitfully. It emphatically denies and condemns God. Again, it makes murder and injustice a good work, a divine service. It puts the devil with his falsehoods in the place of God. It institutes the worst form of idolatry and ruins body and soul, destroying the former by hunger and the latter by a terrified conscience. It makes of God the devil, and of the devil God. It makes hell of heaven, and heaven of hell; righteousness of sin, and sin of righteousness. This I call perversion—where strictest justice is the most strenuous wrong. To this depravity Ezekiel has reference (Ezekiel 13:18–19):

> Thus saith the Lord Jehovah: Woe to the women that sew pillows upon all elbows, and make kerchiefs for the head of persons of every stature to hunt souls! Will ye hunt the souls of my people, and save souls alive for yourselves? And ye have profaned me among my people for handfuls of barley and for pieces of bread, to slay the souls that should not die, and to save the souls alive that should not live, by your lying to my people that hearken unto lies.

What is meant but that the blind teachers of the Law terrify the conscience, and put sin and death in the place of grace and life, and grace and life where is only sin and death; and all for a handful of barley and a bit of bread? In other words, such teachers devote themselves to laws concerning strictly external matters, things that perish with the using, such as a drink of water and a morsel of bread, wholly neglecting love and harassing the conscience with fear of sin unto eternal death; as Ezekiel goes on to say (13: 22–23): "Because with lies ye have grieved the heart of the righteous, whom I have not made sad, and strengthened the hands of the wicked, that he should not return from his wicked way, and be saved alive; therefore ye shall no more see false visions, nor divine divinations: and I will deliver my people out of your hand; and ye shall know that I am Jehovah."

12. Mark you, it is making the hearts of the righteous sad to load them with sins when their works are good; it is strengthening the hands of the wicked to make their works good when they are naught but sin. Relative to this subject, we read (Psalm 14:5): "There were they in great fear; for God is in the generation of the righteous." That is, the sting of conscience fills with fear where there is neither reason for fear nor for a disturbed conscience. That is feared as sin which is really noble service to God. The thought of the last passage is: When they should call upon God and serve Him, they fear such conduct is sin and not divine service; again, when they have need to fear a service not divine, they are secure and unafraid. Isaiah's words (Isaiah 29:13) are to the same effect: "Their fear of me is a commandment of men which hath been taught them." Always the perverted people spoken of corrupt everything. They confidently call on God where is only the devil; they refrain in fear from calling on God where God is.

13. Such, mark you, is the wretched condition of them who are blindly occupied with laws and works and fail to comprehend the design of law and its mistress Love. Note, also, in the case of our miserable ecclesiasts and their followers, how rigidly they adhere to their own inventions! Though all the world meet ruin, their devices must be sustained; they must be perpetuated regardless of bodily illness and death, or of suffering and ruin for the soul. They even regard such destruction and ruin as divine service, and know no fear nor remorse of conscience. Indeed, so strongly entrenched are they in their wicked-

ness, they will never return from it. Moreover, should one of their wretched number be permitted to alleviate the distress of his body and soul—to eat meat, to marry—he is afraid, he feels remorse of conscience; he is uncertain about sin and law, about death and hell; he calls not on God, nor serves Him; all this, even though the body should die ten deaths and the soul go to the devil a hundred times.

14. Observe, then, the state of the world; how little flesh and blood can accomplish even in their best efforts; how dangerous to undertake to rule by law alone—indeed, how impossible it is, without great danger, to govern and instruct souls with mere laws, ignoring love and the Spirit, in whose hands is the full power of all law. It is written (Deuteronomy 33:2), "At his right hand was a fiery law for them." This is the law of love in the Spirit. It shall regulate all laws at the left hand; that is, the external laws of the world. It is said (Exodus 28:30) that the priest must bear upon his breast, in the breastplate, "the Urim and the Thummim"; that is, Light and Perfection, indicative of the priest's office to illuminate the Law—to give its true sense—and faultlessly to keep and to teach it.

15. In the conception, the establishment, and the observance of all laws, the object should be, not the furtherance of the laws in themselves, not the advancement of works, but the exercise of love. That is the true purpose of law, according to Paul here: "He that loveth his neighbor hath fulfilled the law." Therefore, when the law contributes to the injury rather than the benefit of our neighbor, it should be ignored. The same law may at one time benefit our neighbor and at another time injure him. Consequently, it should be regulated according to its advantage to him. Law should be made to serve in the same way that food and raiment and other necessaries of life serve. We consider not the food and raiment themselves, but their benefit to our needy neighbor. And we cease to dispense them as soon as we perceive they no longer add to his comfort.

16. Suppose you were to come across an individual foolish enough to act with no other thought than that food and clothing are truly good things, and so proceed to stuff a needy one with unlimited food and drink unto choking, and to clothe him unto suffocation, and then not to desist. Suppose to the command, "Stop, you have suffocated, have already over-fed and over-clothed him, and all is lost effort now," the foolish one should reply: "You heretic, would you forbid good works? Food, drink, and raiment are good things; therefore, we must not cease to dispense them; we cannot do too much." And suppose he continued to force food and clothing on the man. Tell me, what would you think of such a one? He is a fool more than foolish; he is more mad than madness itself. But such is about the character of our ecclesiasts today, and of those who are so blind in the exercise of law as to act as if works were the only requisite, and to suffocate body and soul, being ignorant that the one purpose of law is to call forth the exercise of love. They make works superior to love, and a maid to her matron. Such perversion prevails to an extent distressing to think of, not to mention hearing and seeing it, or more, practicing and permitting it ourselves.

17. The commandment of love is not a long one; it is short. It is one injunction, not many. It is even not a commandment, and at the same time is all commandments. Brief, and a unit in itself, its meaning is easily comprehended. But in its exercise, it is far-reaching, for it includes and regulates all commandments. So far as works are enjoined, it is no commandment at all; it names no peculiar work. Yet it represents all commandments, because properly the fulfillment of all commandments is the fulfillment of this. The commandment of love suspends every commandment, yet it perpetuates all. Its whole purpose is that we may recognize no commandment, no work, except as love dictates.

18. As life on earth apart from works is an impossibility, necessarily there must be various commandments involving works. Yet love is supreme over these requirements, dictating the omission or the per-

formance of works according to its own best interests, and permitting no works opposed to itself.

To illustrate: A driver, holding the reins, guides team and wagon at will. If he were content merely to hold the reins, regardless of whether the team followed the road, the entire equipage—team, wagon, reins, and driver—would soon be wrecked; the driver would be lying drowned in a ditch or a pool, or have his neck broken going over stumps and rocks. But if he dextrously regulates the movement of the outfit according to the road, observing where it is safe and where unsafe, he will proceed securely because wisely. Were he, in his egotism, to drive straight ahead, endeavoring to make the road conform to the movement of the wagon, at his pleasure, he would soon see how beautifully his plan would work.

19. So it is when men are governed by laws and works, the laws not being regulated according to the people. The case is that of the driver who would regulate the road by the movements of the wagon. True, the road is often well suited to the straight course of the wagon. But just as truly the road is, in certain places, crooked and uneven, and then the wagon must conform to the course and condition of the road. Men must adapt themselves to laws and regulations wherever possible and where the laws are beneficial. But where laws prove detrimental to men's interests, the former must yield. The ruler must wisely make allowance for love, suspending works and laws. Hence, philosophers say prudence—or circumspection or discretion as the ecclesiasts put it—is the guide and regulator of all virtues.

20. We read in a book of the ancient fathers that on a certain occasion of their assembling, the question was raised, which is really the noblest work? Various replies were given. One said prayer, another fasting; but St. Anthony was of the opinion that of all works and virtues, discretion is the best and surest way to heaven. These, however, were but childish, unspiritual ideas relating to their own chosen works. A

Christian views the matter in quite a different light, and more judiciously. He concludes that neither discretion nor rashness avails before God. Only faith and love serve with Him. But love is true discretion; love is the driver and the true discretion in righteous works. It always looks to the good of the neighbor, to the amelioration of his condition; just as the discretion of the world looks to the general welfare of the governed in the adjustment of political laws. Let this suffice on this point.

21. But the question arises: How can love fulfill the Law when love is but one of the fruits of faith and we have frequently said that only faith in Christ removes our sins, justifies us, and satisfies all the demands of the Law? How can we make the two claims harmonize? Christ says, too (Matthew 7:12): "All things, therefore, whatsoever ye would that men should do unto you, even so do ye also unto them: for this is the law and the prophets." Thus He shows that love for one's neighbor fulfills both the Law and the Prophets. Again, He says (Matthew 22:37–40): "Thou shalt love the Lord thy God . . . thy neighbor as thyself. On these two the whole law hangeth, and the prophets." Where, then, does Paul stand, who says (Romans 3:31): "Do we then make the law of none effect through faith? God forbid: nay, we establish the law." Again (Romans 3:28): "We reckon therefore that a man is justified by faith apart from the works of the law." And again (Romans 1:17):"The righteous shall live by faith."

22. I reply: As we have frequently said, we must properly distinguish between faith and love. Faith deals with the heart, and love with the works. Faith removes our sins, renders us acceptable, justifies us. And being accepted and justified as to our person, love is given us in the Holy Spirit and we delight in doing good. Now, it is the nature of the Law to attack our person and demand good works; and it will not cease to demand until it gains its point. We cannot do good works without the Spirit and love. The Law constrains us to know ourselves with our imperfections, and to recognize the necessity of our becom-

ing altogether different individuals that we may satisfy the Law. The Law does not exact so much of the heart as of works; in fact, it demands nothing but works and ignores the heart. It leaves the individual to discover, from the works required, that he must become an altogether different person. But faith, when it comes, creates a nature capable of accomplishing the works the Law demands. Thus is the Law fulfilled.

So Paul's sayings on the subject are beautiful and appropriate. The Law demands of us works; it must be fulfilled by works. Hence it cannot in every sense be said that faith fulfills the Law. However, it prepares the way and enables us to fulfill it, for the Law demands, not us, but our works. The Law constrains us—teaches us that we must be changed before we can accomplish its works; it makes us conscious of our inability as we are. On the other hand, love and works do not change us, do not justify us. We must be changed in person and justified before we can love and do good works. Our love and our works are evidence of justification and of a change, since they are impossible until the individual is free from sin and made righteous.

23. This explanation is given to enable us to perceive the true nature of the Law, of faith, and of love; to ascribe to each its own mission; and rightly to understand the Scripture declarations in their harmonious relations that while faith justifies, it does not fulfill the Law, and that while love does not justify, it does fulfill the Law. The Law requires love and works, but does not mention the heart. The heart is sensible of the Law, but love is not. Just as the Law, in requiring works before faith exists, is a sign to the individual leading him to recognize his utter lack of faith and righteousness, and to conclude he is conquered, so love in its fulfillment of the Law after faith intervenes is a sign and a proof to the individual of his faith and righteousness. Law and love, then, witness to him concerning his unrighteousness or his righteousness. After faith comes, love is evidence of righteousness.

Before faith, man is sensible of the Law's oppression because he knows he does not possess what the Law requires. And the Law does not require a changed heart, but works. Love and works do not effect the fulfillment of the Law; they are themselves its fulfillment.

24. Now, though faith does not fulfill the Law, it contains that which effects its fulfillment; it secures the Spirit and love whereby the end is accomplished. On the other hand, if love does not justify us, it makes manifest the faith whereby we are justified. Briefly, as Paul says here, "Love is the fulfillment of the law." His thought is: Fulfillment of the Law is one thing, and effecting or furnishing its fulfillment another. Love fulfills the Law in the sense that love itself is its fulfillment; but faith fulfills it in the sense that it offers that by which it is fulfilled. For faith loves and works, as said in Galatians 5:6, "Faith worketh through love." The water fills the pitcher; so does the cup-bearer. The water fills of itself; the cupbearer fills with the water—"effective et formaliter implere," as the sophists would say.

25. Faith is ever the actor, and love the act. The Law requires the act and thus forces the actor to be changed. The Law is then fulfilled by the act, which, however, the actor must perform. Thus Paul rejects the fancies of the sophists, who in the matter of love would make a distinction between the external work and the inner affection, saying: "Love is an inner affection that loves our neighbor when in our heart we wish him well." Its expression in works, however, they call the fruit of love. But we will not discuss this idea. Note, Paul terms love not only an affection, but an affectionate good act. Faith and the heart are the actor and fulfiller of the Law. Paul says, "He that loveth his neighbor hath fulfilled the law." And love is the act, the fulfilling; for he says, "Love is the fulfillment of the law."

26. Another question arises: How can love for our neighbor be the fulfillment of the Law when we are required to love God supremely, even above our neighbor? I reply: Christ answers the question when He

tells us (Matthew 22:39) the second commandment is like unto the first. He makes love to God and love to our neighbor the same love. The reason for this is, first: God, having no need for our works and benefactions for Himself, bids us to do for our neighbor what we would do for God. He asks for Himself only our faith and our recognition of Him as God. The object of proclaiming His honor and rendering Him praise and thanks here on earth is that our neighbor may be converted and brought into fellowship with God. Such service is called the love of God and is performed out of love to God; but it is exercised for the benefit of our neighbor only.

27. The second reason why God makes love to our neighbor an obligation equal to love to Himself is: God has made worldly wisdom foolish, desiring henceforth to be loved amid crosses and afflictions. Paul says (1 Corinthians 1:21), "Seeing that in the wisdom of God the world through its wisdom knew not God, it was God's good pleasure through the foolishness of the preaching to save them that believe." Therefore, upon the cross He submitted Himself unto death and misery, and imposed the same submission upon all His disciples. They who refused to love Him before when He bestowed upon them food and drink, blessing and honor, must now love Him in hunger and sorrow, in adversity and disgrace. All works of love, then, must be directed to our wretched, needy neighbors. In these lowly ones we are to find and love God, in them we are to serve and honor Him, and only so can we do it. The commandment to love God is wholly merged in that to love our neighbors.

28. These facts restrain those elusive, soaring spirits that seek after God only in great and glorious undertakings. It stops the mouths of those who strive after greatness like His, who would force themselves into heaven, presuming to serve and love Him with their brilliant works. But they miss Him by passing over Him in their earthly neighbor, in whom God would be loved and honored. Therefore, they will

hear, on the last day, the sentence (Matthew 25:42), "I was hungry, and ye did not give me to eat," etc. For Christ laid aside his divinity and took upon Himself the form of a servant for the very purpose of bringing down and centering upon our neighbor the love we extend to Himself. Yet we leave the Lord to lie here in His humiliation while we gaze open-mouthed into heaven and make great pretensions to love and service to God.

ALL COMMANDMENTS SUMMED UP IN LOVE

For this, Thou shalt not commit adultery, Thou shalt not kill,
Thou shalt not steal, Thou shalt not covet; and if there be any other
commandment, it is briefly summed up in this word, namely,
Thou shalt love thy neighbor as thyself.

29. Love being the chief element of all law, it comprehends, as has been made sufficiently clear, all commandments. Its one concern is to be useful to man and not harmful; therefore, it readily discovers the way. Recognizing the fact that man, from his ardent self-love, seeks to promote his own interests and avoid injuring them, love endeavors to adopt the same course toward others. We will consider the commandment just cited, noticing how ingeniously and wisely it is arranged. It brings out four thoughts. First, it states who is under obligation to love: thou—the nearest, noblest, best individual we can command. No one can fulfill the Law of God for another; each must do it for himself. As Paul says (Galatians 6:5), "Each man shall bear his own burden." And (2 Corinthians 5:10): "For we must all be made manifest before the judgment-seat of Christ; that each one may receive the things done in the body, according to what he hath done, whether it be good or bad." So it is said, "Thou, thou thyself, must love"; not, "Let someone else love for you." Though one can and should pray that God may be gracious to

another and help him, yet no one will be saved unless he himself fulfills God's command. It is not enough merely to pray that another may escape punishment, as the venders of indulgences teach; much rather, we should pray that he become righteous and observe God's precepts.

30. Second, the commandment names the noblest virtue—love. It does not say, "Thou shalt feed thy neighbor, give him drink, clothe him," all of which things are inestimably good works; it says, "Thou shalt love him." Love is the chief virtue, the fountain of all virtues. Love gives food and drink; it clothes, comforts, persuades, relieves, and rescues. What shall we say of it, for behold, he who loves gives himself, body and soul, property and honor, all his powers inner and external, for his needy neighbor's benefit, whether it be friend or enemy; he withholds nothing wherewith he may serve another. There is no virtue like love; there can be no special work assigned it as in the case of limited virtues, such as chastity, mercy, patience, meekness, and the like. Love does all things. It will suffer in life and in death, in every condition, and that even for its enemies. Well may Paul here say that all other commandments are briefly comprehended in the injunction, "Thou shalt love thy neighbor as thyself."

31. Third, the commandment names, as the sphere of our love, the noblest field, the dearest friend—our neighbor. It does not say, "Thou shalt love the rich, the mighty, the learned, the saint." No, the unrestrained love designated in this most perfect commandment does not apportion itself among the few. With it is no respect of persons. It is the nature of false, carnal, worldly love to respect the individual, and to love only so long as it hopes to derive profit. When such hope ceases, that love also ceases. The commandment of our text, however, requires of us free, spontaneous love to all men, whoever they may be, and whether friend or foe, a love that seeks not profit, and administers only what is beneficial. Such love is most active and powerful in serving the poor, the needy, the sick, the wicked, the simpleminded, and

the hostile; among these it is always and under all circumstances necessary to suffer and endure, to serve and do good.

32. Note here, this commandment makes us all equal before God, without regard to distinctions incident to our stations in life, to our persons, offices, and occupations. Since the commandment is to all—to every human being—a sovereign, if he be a human being, must confess the poorest beggar, the most wretched leper, his neighbor and his equal in the sight of God. He is under obligation, according to this commandment, not to extend a measure of help, but to serve that neighbor with all he has and all he controls. If he loves him as God here commands him to do, he must give the beggar preference over his crown and all his realm; and if the beggar's necessity requires, must give his life. He is under obligation to love his neighbor, and must admit that such a one is his neighbor.

33. Is not this a superior, a noble, commandment, which completely levels the most unequal individuals? Is it not wonderfully comforting to the beggar to have servants and lovers of such honor? wonderful that his poverty commands the services of a king in his opulence? that to his sores and wounds are subject the crown of wealth and the sweet savor of royal splendor? But how strange it would seem to us to behold kings and queens, princes and princesses, serving beggars and lepers, as we read St. Elizabeth did! Even this, however, would be a slight thing in comparison with what Christ has done. No one can ever equal Him in the obedience wherewith He has exalted this commandment. He is a king whose honor transcends that of all other kings; indeed, He is the Son of God. And yet He puts himself on a level with the worst sinners, and serves them even to dying for them. Were ten kings of earth to serve to the utmost one beggar, it would be a remarkable thing; but of what significance would it be in comparison with the service Christ has rendered? The kings would be put to utter shame and would have to acknowledge their service unworthy of notice.

34. Learn, then, the condition of the world—how far it is not only from Christ's immeasurable example, but from commandment in this verse. Where are to be found any who comprehend the meaning of the little phrase "thy neighbor," notwithstanding there is, beside this commandment, the natural law of service written in the hearts of all men? Not an individual is there who does not realize, and who is not forced to confess, the justice and truth of the natural law outlined in the command (Matthew 7:12), "All things therefore whatsoever ye would that men should do unto you, even so do ye also unto them." The light of this law shines in the inborn reason of all men. Did they but regard it, what need have they of books, teachers, or laws? They carry with them in the depths of their hearts a living book, fitted to teach them fully what to do and what to omit, what to accept and what to reject, and what decision to make.

Now, the command to love our neighbors as ourselves is equivalent to that other, "Whatsoever ye would that men should do unto you," etc. Every individual desires to be loved and not hated; and he also feels and sees his obligation to exercise the same disposition toward others. The carrying out of this obligation is loving another as himself. But evil lust and sinful love obscure the light of natural law, and blind man, until he fails to perceive the guidebook in his heart and to follow the clear command of reason. Hence he must be restrained and repelled by external laws and material books, with the sword and by force. He must be reminded of his natural light and have his own heart revealed to him. Yet admonition does not avail; he does not see the light. Evil lust and sinful love blind him. With the sword and with political laws he must still be outwardly restrained from perpetrating actual crimes.

35. The fourth thing the commandment presents is the standard by which we are to measure our love—an excellent model. Those are particularly worthy instructions and commandments which present

examples. This commandment holds up a truly living example—"thyself." It is a better model than any example the saints have set. The saints are dead and their deeds are past, but this example ever lives. Everyone must admit a consciousness of his own love for himself; of his ardent concern for his temporal life; of his careful nourishment of his body with food, raiment, and all good things; of his fleeing from death and avoiding evil. This is self-love; something we are conscious of in ourselves. What, then, is the teaching of the commandment? To do to another as you do to yourself; to value his body and his life equally with your own body and life. Now, how could God have pointed you to an example dearer, more pleasing, and more to the purpose than this example—the deep instinct of your nature? Indeed, your depth of character is measured by the writing of this command in your heart.

36. How will you fare with God if you do not love your neighbor? Feeling this commandment written within your heart, your conscience will condemn you. Your whole conduct will be an example witnessing against you, testifying to your failure to do unto others as the natural instinct of your being, more forcibly than all the examples of the saints, has taught you to do. But how will it go with the ecclesiasts in particular—the churchmen with their singing and praying, their cowls and bald pates, and all their jugglery? I make no comment on the fact that they have never observed the commandment. I ask, however, when has their monastic fanaticism permitted them time and opportunity to perceive for once this law in their hearts, to become sensible of the example set them in their own human instinct, or even to read the precept in books or hear it preached? Poor, miserable people! Do you presume to think that God will make void this, love's commandment, so deeply and clearly impressed upon the heart, so beautifully and unmistakably illustrated in your own natures, and in the many written and spoken words as well—think you God will

do this on account of your cowls and bald pates, and regard what you have been devising and performing?

37. Alas, how shamelessly the world has ignored this beautiful and impressive commandment wherein are so skillfully presented the individual, the task, the model, and the sphere of labor! And, on the other hand, how shamefully it occupies itself with the very reverse of what is taught in this commandment! Its whole practice and tendency seem to be to place our responsibility upon others; monks and priests must be righteous for us and pray in our stead, that we may personally be excused. For the noblest virtue, love, we substitute self-devised works; in the place of our neighbors we put wood and stone, raiment and food, even dead souls—the saints of heaven. These we serve; with them we are occupied; they are the sphere wherein we exercise ourselves. Instead of the noblest example—"as thyself"—we look to the legends and the works of saints. We presume to imitate such outward examples, omitting the duty which our own nature and life present and which the command of God outlines, notwithstanding such duty offers more than we could ever fulfil. Even if we could accomplish all it offers, we would still not equal Christ.

LOVE WORKS ONLY GOOD TO ITS NEIGHBOR

Love worketh no ill to his neighbor: love, therefore,
is the fulfilment of the law.

38. The Ten Commandments forbid doing evil to our neighbor— "Thou shalt not kill, Thou shalt not commit adultery," etc. The apostle, employing similar phraseology, says that love observes all these commands, injuring none. Not only that; it effects good for all. It is practically doing evil to permit our neighbor to remain in peril when we can relieve him, even though we may not have been instrumental in

placing him where he is. If he is hungry and we do not feed him when it is in our power to do so, we practically permit him to die of hunger. We should take this view concerning any perilous condition, any adverse circumstance, with our neighbors. How love is the fulfillment of the Law, we have now heard.

This sermon was taken from volume 7, pages 56–75, of The Sermons of Martin Luther *[Grand Rapids, MI: Baker Book House]. It was originally published in 1909 in English by the Luther Press [Minneapolis, MN], as* Luther's Epistle Sermons, *vol. 2. The pagination from the Baker edition has been maintained for referencing. This e-text was scanned and edited by Richard P. Bucher. It is in the public domain and may be copied and distributed without restriction.)*

6

Max Lucado

ROCKING THE BOAT

═══════════

Max Lucado (1955–) is an author, a speaker, and the pastor of Oak Hills Church in San Antonio, Texas. Some of his books include The Applause of Heaven, In the Grip of Grace, Traveling Light, *and* Come Thirsty.

The following excerpt from In the The Grip of Grace *discusses biblical unity.*

God has enlisted us in his navy and placed us on his ship. The boat has one purpose—to carry us safely to the other shore.

This is no cruise ship; it's a battleship. We aren't called to a life of leisure; we are called to a life of service. Each of us has a different task. Some, concerned with those who are drowning, are snatching people from the water. Others are occupied with the enemy, so they man the cannons of prayer and worship. Still others devote themselves to the crew, feeding and training the crew members.

Though different, we are the same. Each can tell of a personal encounter with the captain, for each has received a personal call. He found us among the shanties of the seaport and invited us to follow

Him. Our faith was born at the sight of His fondness, and so we went.

We each followed Him across the gangplank of His grace onto the same boat. There is one captain and one destination. Though the battle is fierce, the boat is safe, for our captain is God. The ship will not sink. For that, there is no concern.

There is concern, however, regarding the disharmony of the crew. When we first boarded we assumed the crew was made up of others like us. But as we've wandered these decks, we've encountered curious converts with curious appearances. Some wear uniforms we've never seen, sporting styles we've never witnessed. "Why do you look the way you do?" we ask them.

"Funny," they reply. "We were about to ask the same of you." The variety of dress is not nearly as disturbing as the plethora of opinions. There is a group, for example, who clusters every morning for serious study. They promote rigid discipline and somber expressions. "Serving the captain is serious business," they explain. It's no coincidence that they tend to congregate around the stern. There is another regiment deeply devoted to prayer. Not only do they believe in prayer; they believe in prayer by kneeling. For that reason you always know where to locate them; they are at the bow of the ship.

And then there are a few who staunchly believe real wine should be used in the Lord's Supper. You'll find them on the port side. Still another group has positioned themselves near the engine. They spend hours examining the nuts and bolts of the boat. They've been known to go below deck and not come up for days. They are occasionally criticized by those who linger on the top deck, feeling the wind in their hair and the sun on their face. "It's not what you learn," those topside argue. "It's what you feel that matters."

And, oh, how we tend to cluster.

Some think once you're on the boat, you can't get off. Others say you'd be foolish to go overboard, but the choice is yours.

Some believe you volunteer for service; others believe you were destined for the service before the ship was even built.

Some predict a storm of great tribulation will strike before we dock; others say it won't hit until we are safely ashore.

There are those who speak to the captain in a personal language. There are those who think such languages are extinct.

There are those who think the officers should wear robes, there are those who think there should be no officers at all, and there are those who think we are all officers and should all wear robes.

And, oh, how we tend to cluster.

And then there is the issue of the weekly meeting at which the captain is thanked and His words are read. All agree on its importance, but few agree on its nature. Some want it loud, others quiet. Some want ritual, others spontaneity. Some want to celebrate so they can meditate; others meditate so they can celebrate. Some want a meeting for those who've gone overboard. Others want to reach those overboard but without going overboard and neglecting those on board.

And, oh, how we tend to cluster.

The consequence is a rocky boat. There is trouble on deck. Fights have broken out. Sailors have refused to speak to each other. There have even been times when one group refused to acknowledge the presence of others on the ship. Most tragically, some adrift at sea have chosen not to board the boat because of the quarreling of the sailors.

"What do we do?" we'd like to ask the captain. "How can there be harmony on the ship?" We don't have to go far to find the answer.

On the last night of His life, Jesus prayed a prayer that stands as a citadel for all Christians:

> I pray for these followers, but I am also praying for all those who
> will believe in me because of their teaching. Father, I pray that

they can be one. As you are in me and I am in you, I pray that they can also be one in us. Then the world will believe that you sent me. (John 17:20–21 NCV)

How precious are these words. Jesus, knowing the end is near, prays one final time for His followers. Striking, isn't it, that He prayed not for their success, their safety, or their happiness.

He prayed for their unity. He prayed that they would love each other.

As He prayed for them, He also prayed for "those who will believe . . . because of their teaching." That means us! In His last prayer Jesus prayed that you and I be one.

Of all the lessons we can draw from this verse, don't miss the most important: unity matters to God. The Father does not want His kids to squabble. Disunity disturbs Him. Why? Because "all people will know that you are my followers if you love each other" (John 13:35 NCV). Unity creates belief. How will the world believe that Jesus was sent by God? Not if we agree with each other. Not if we solve every controversy. Not if we are unanimous on each vote. Not if we never make a doctrinal error. But if we love one another.

Unity creates belief. Disunity fosters disbelief. Who wants to board a ship of bickering sailors? Life on the ocean may be rough, but at least the waves don't call us names.

Reprinted with permission from Max Lucado, In the Grip of Grace *[Nashville: Word Publishing, 2001].*

7

The Prophet Isaiah

GOD'S PEOPLE ARE COMFORTED

Isaiah—a prophet of the Old Testament—is often thought of as the greatest of all writing prophets in the Bible. His name means "the Lord saves."

"Comfort, yes, comfort My people!"
Says your God.
"Speak comfort to Jerusalem, and cry out to her,
That her warfare is ended,
That her iniquity is pardoned;
For she has received from the LORD's hand
Double for all her sins."

The voice of one crying in the wilderness:
"Prepare the way of the LORD;
Make straight in the desert
A highway for our God.
Every valley shall be exalted
And every mountain and hill brought low;
The crooked places shall be made straight

And the rough places smooth;
The glory of the LORD shall be revealed,
And all flesh shall see it together;
For the mouth of the LORD has spoken."

The voice said, "Cry out!"
And he said, "What shall I cry?"

"All flesh is grass,
And all its loveliness is like the flower of the field.
The grass withers, the flower fades,
Because the breath of the LORD blows upon it;
Surely the people are grass.
The grass withers, the flower fades,
But the word of our God stands forever."

O Zion,
You who bring good tidings,
Get up into the high mountain;
O Jerusalem,
You who bring good tidings,
Lift up your voice with strength,
Lift it up, be not afraid;
Say to the cities of Judah, "Behold your God!"

Behold, the Lord GOD shall come with a strong hand,
And His arm shall rule for Him;
Behold, His reward is with Him,
And His work before Him.
He will feed His flock like a shepherd;
He will gather the lambs with His arm,

And carry them in His bosom,
And gently lead those who are with young.

Who has measured the waters in the hollow of his hand,
Measured heaven with a span
And calculated the dust of the earth in a measure?
Weighed the mountains in scales
And the hills in a balance?
Who has directed the Spirit of the LORD,
Or as His counselor has taught Him?
With whom did He take counsel, and who instructed Him,
And taught Him in the path of justice?
Who taught Him knowledge,
And showed Him the way of understanding?

Behold, the nations are as a drop in a bucket,
And are counted as the small dust on the scales;
Look, He lifts up the isles as a very little thing.
And Lebanon is not sufficient to burn,
Nor its beasts sufficient for a burnt offering.
All nations before Him are as nothing,
And they are counted by Him less than nothing and worthless.
To whom then will you liken God?
Or what likeness will you compare to Him?
The workman molds an image,
The goldsmith overspreads it with gold,
And the silversmith casts silver chains.
Whoever is too impoverished for such a contribution
Chooses a tree that will not rot;
He seeks for himself a skillful workman
To prepare a carved image that will not totter.

Have you not known?
Have you not heard?
Has it not been told you from the beginning?
Have you not understood from the foundations of the earth?
It is He who sits above the circle of the earth,
And its inhabitants are like grasshoppers,
Who stretches out the heavens like a curtain,
And spreads them out like a tent to dwell in.
He brings the princes to nothing;
He makes the judges of the earth useless.

Scarcely shall they be planted,
Scarcely shall they be sown,
Scarcely shall their stock take root in the earth,
When He will also blow on them,
And they will wither,
And the whirlwind will take them away like stubble.

"To whom then will you liken Me,
Or to whom shall I be equal?" says the Holy One.
Lift up your eyes on high,
And see who has created these things,
Who brings out their host by number;
He calls them all by name,
By the greatness of His might
And the strength of His power;
Not one is missing.

Why do you say, O Jacob,
And speak, O Israel:
"My way is hidden from the LORD,

And my just claim is passed over by my God"?
Have you not known?
Have you not heard?
The everlasting God, the LORD,
The Creator of the ends of the earth,
Neither faints nor is weary.
His understanding is unsearchable.
He gives power to the weak,
And to those who have no might He increases strength.
Even the youths shall faint and be weary,
And the young men shall utterly fall,
But those who wait on the LORD
Shall renew their strength;
They shall mount up with wings like eagles,
They shall run and not be weary,
They shall walk and not faint.

Isaiah 40, NKJV.

8

Mother Teresa

WHATSOEVER YOU DO . . .

═══════════

Mother Teresa (1910–1997) was born in Skopje, Macedonia. On October 7, 1950, Mother Teresa received permission from the Holy See to start her own order, the "Missionaries of Charity," whose primary task was to love and care for those persons nobody was prepared to look after. She is most noted for her acts of service to the impoverished people of Calcutta.

The following speech was delivered by Mother Teresa at the National Prayer Breakfast in Washington, D.C., on February 3, 1994.

On the last day, Jesus will say to those on His right hand, "Come, enter the kingdom. For I was hungry and you gave Me food, I was thirsty and you gave Me drink, I was sick and you visited Me." Then Jesus will turn to those on His left hand and say, "Depart from Me, because I was hungry and you did not feed Me, I was thirsty and you did not give Me drink, I was sick and you did not visit Me." These will ask Him, "When did we see You hungry or thirsty or sick and did not come to Your help?" And Jesus will answer them, "Whatever you neglected to do unto one of the least of these, you neglected to do unto Me!"

As we have gathered here to pray together, I think it will be beautiful if we begin with a prayer that expressed very well what Jesus wants us to do for the least. St. Francis of Assisi understood very well these words of Jesus, and His life is very well expressed by a prayer. And this prayer, which we say every day after Holy Communion, always surprises me very much, because it is very fitting for each one of us. And I always wonder whether eight hundred years ago when St. Francis lived, they had the same difficulties that we have today. I think that some of you already have this prayer of peace—so we will pray it together.

> Lord, make me an instrument of Your peace. Where there is hatred let me sow love, where there is injury let me sow pardon, where there is doubt let me sow faith, where there is despair let me give hope, where there is darkness let me give light, where there is sadness let me give joy. O Divine Master, grant that I may not try to be comforted but to comfort, not try to be understood but to understand, not try to be loved but to love. Because it is in giving that we receive, it is in forgiving that we are forgiven, and it is in dying that we are born to eternal life.

Let us thank God for the opportunity He has given us today to have come here to pray together. We have come here especially to pray for peace, joy, and love. We are reminded that Jesus came to bring the good news to the poor. He had told us what that good news is when He said: "My peace I leave with you, My peace I give unto you." He came not to give the peace of the world, which is only that we don't bother each other. He came to give the peace of heart which comes from loving—from doing good to others.

And God loved the world so much that He gave His Son—it was

a giving. God gave His Son to the Virgin Mary, and what did she do with Him? As soon as Jesus came into Mary's life, immediately she went in haste to give that good news. And as she came into the house of her cousin, Elizabeth, Scripture tells us that the unborn child—the child in the womb of Elizabeth—leapt with joy. While still in the womb of Mary, Jesus brought peace to John the Baptist, who leapt for joy in the womb of Elizabeth.

And as if that were not enough, as if it were not enough that God the Son should become one of us and bring peace and joy while still in the womb of Mary, Jesus also died on the cross to show that greater love. He died for you and for me, and for that leper and for that man dying of hunger and that naked person lying in the street, not only of Calcutta, but of Africa, and everywhere. Our Sisters serve these poor people in 105 countries throughout the world. Jesus insisted that we love one another as He loves each one of us.

Jesus gave His life to love us, and He tells us that we also have to give whatever it takes to do good to one another. And in the Gospel Jesus says very clearly: "Love as I have loved you." Jesus died on the cross because that is what it took for Him to do good to us—to save us from our selfishness in sin. He gave up everything to do the Father's will to show us that we, too, must be willing to give up everything to do God's will—to love one another as He loves each of us. If we are not willing to give whatever it takes to do good to one another, sin is still in us. That is why we, too, must give to each other until it hurts.

It is not enough for us to say, "I love God," but I also have to love my neighbor. St. John says that you are a liar if you say you love God and you don't love your neighbor.

How can you love God, whom you do not see, if you do not love your neighbor, whom you see, whom you touch, with whom you live?

And so it is very important for us to realize that love, to be true, has to hurt. I must be willing to give whatever it takes not to harm other people and, in fact, to do good to them. This requires that I be willing to give until it hurts. Otherwise, there is no true love in me and I bring injustice, not peace, to those around me.

It hurt Jesus to love us. We have been created in His image for greater things, to love and to be loved. We must "put on Christ" as Scripture tells us. And so we have been created to love and to be loved, and God has become man to make it possible for us to love as He loved us. Jesus makes Himself the hungry one, the naked one, the homeless one, the unwanted one, and He says, "You did it to Me." On the last day He will say to those on His right, "Whatever you did to the least of these, you did to Me," and He will also say to those on His left, "Whatever you neglected to do for the least of these, you neglected to do it for Me."

When He was dying on the cross, Jesus said, "I thirst." Jesus is thirsting for our love, and this is the thirst of everyone, poor and rich alike. We all thirst for the love of others, that they go out of their way to avoid harming us and to do good to us. This is the meaning of true love, to give until it hurts.

I can never forget the experience I had in visiting a home where they kept all these old parents of sons and daughters who had just put them into an institution and forgotten them—maybe. I saw that in that home these old people had everything—good food, comfortable place, television, everything, but everyone was looking toward the door. And I did not see a single one with a smile on the face. I turned to Sister and I asked: "Why do these people who have every comfort here, why are they all looking toward the door? Why are they not smiling?"

I am so used to seeing the smiles on our people; even the dying ones smile.

And Sister said: "This is the way it is nearly every day. They are expecting, they are hoping that a son or daughter will come to visit them. They are hurt because they are forgotten." And see, this neglect to love brings spiritual poverty. Maybe in our own family we have somebody who is feeling lonely, who is feeling sick, who is feeling worried. Are we there? Are we there to be with them, or do we merely put them in the care of others? Are we willing to give until it hurts in order to be with our families, or do we put our own interests first? These are the questions we must ask ourselves, especially as we begin this year of the family. We must remember that love begins at home, and we must also remember that "the future of humanity passes through the family."

I was surprised in the West to see so many young boys and girls given to drugs. And I tried to find out why. Why is it like that, when those in the West have so many more things than those in the East? And the answer was: "Because there is no one in the family to receive them." Our children depend on us for everything—their health, their nutrition, their security, their coming to know and love God. For all of this, they look to us with trust, hope, and expectation. But often father and mother are so busy they have no time for their children, or perhaps they are not even married or have given up on their marriage. So the children go to the streets and get involved in drugs or other things. We are talking of love of the child, which is where love and peace must begin. These are the things that break peace.

But I feel that the greatest destroyer of peace today is abortion, because it is a war against the child, a direct killing of the innocent child, murder by the mother herself.

And if we accept that a mother can kill even her own child, how can we tell other people not to kill one another? How do we persuade a woman not to have an abortion? As always, we must persuade her with love, and we remind ourselves that love means to be willing to give until it hurts. Jesus gave even His life to love us. So the mother who is thinking of abortion should be helped to love, that is, to give until it hurts her plans, or her free time, to respect the life of her child. The father of that child, whoever he is, must also give until it hurts.

By abortion, the mother does not learn to love, but kills even her own child to solve her problems.

And, by abortion, the father is told that he does not have to take any responsibility at all for the child he has brought into the world. That father is likely to put other women into the same trouble. So abortion just leads to more abortion.

Any country that accepts abortion is not teaching its people to love, but to use any violence to get what they want. This is why the greatest destroyer of love and peace is abortion.

Many people are very, very concerned with the children of India, with the children of Africa where quite a few die of hunger, and so on. Many people are also concerned about all the violence in this great country of the United States. These concerns are very good. But often these same people are not concerned with the millions who are being killed by the deliberate decision of their own mothers. And this is what is the greatest destroyer of peace today—abortion, which brings people to such blindness.

And for this I appeal in India and I appeal everywhere—"Let us bring the child back." The child is God's gift to the family. Each child is created in the special image and likeness of God for greater things— to love and to be loved. In this year of the family, we must bring the child back to the center of our care and concern. This is the only way that our world can survive, because our children are the only hope for the future. As older people are called to God, only their children can take their places.

But what does God say to us? He says: "Even if a mother could forget her child, I will not forget you. I have carved you in the palm of My hand." We are carved in the palm of His hand; that unborn child has been carved in the hand of God from conception and is called by

God to love and to be loved, not only now in this life, but forever. God can never forget us.

I will tell you something beautiful. We are fighting abortion by adoption—by care of the mother and adoption for her baby. We have saved thousands of lives. We have sent word to the clinics, to the hospitals and police stations: "Please don't destroy the child; we will take the child." So we always have someone tell the mothers in trouble: "Come, we will take care of you, we will get a home for your child." And we have a tremendous demand from couples who cannot have a child—but I never give a child to a couple who have done something not to have a child. Jesus said. "Anyone who receives a child in My name receives Me." By adopting a child, these couples receive Jesus, but by aborting a child, a couple refuses to receive Jesus.

Please don't kill the child. I want the child. Please give me the child. I am willing to accept any child who would be aborted and to give that child to a married couple who will love the child and be loved by the child.

From our children's home in Calcutta alone, we have saved over three thousand children from abortion. These children have brought such love and joy to their adopting parents and have grown up so full of love and joy.

I know that couples have to plan their family, and for that there is natural family planning.

The way to plan the family is natural family planning, not contraception.

In destroying the power of giving life, through contraception, a husband or wife is doing something to self. This turns the attention to self, and so it destroys the gift of love in him or her. In loving, the husband and wife must turn the attention to each other, as happens in natural family planning, and not to self, as happens in contraception. Once that living love is destroyed by contraception, abortion follows very easily.

I also know that there are great problems in the world—that many spouses do not love each other enough to practice natural family planning. We cannot solve all the problems in the world, but let us never bring in the worst problem of all, and that is to destroy love. And this is what happens when we tell people to practice contraception and abortion.

The poor are very great people. They can teach us so many beautiful things. Once one of them came to thank us for teaching her natural family planning and said: "You people who have practiced chastity, you are the best people to teach us natural family planning, because it is nothing more than self-control out of love for each other." And what this poor person said is very true. These poor people maybe have nothing to eat, maybe they have not a home to live in, but they can still be great people when they are spiritually rich.

When I pick up a person from the street, hungry, I give him a plate of rice, a piece of bread. But a person who is shut out, who feels unwanted, unloved, terrified, the person who has been thrown out of society—that spiritual poverty is much harder to overcome. And abortion, which often follows from contraception, brings a people to be spiritually poor, and that is the worst poverty and the most difficult to overcome.

Those who are materially poor can be very wonderful people. One evening we went out and we picked up four people from the street. And one of them was in a most terrible condition. I told the Sisters: "You take care of the other three; I will take care of the one who looks worse." So I did for her all that my love can do. I put her in bed, and there was such a beautiful smile on her face.

She took hold of my hand as she said one word only: "Thank you"—and she died.

I could not help but examine my conscience before her. And I asked: "What would I say if I were in her place?" And my answer was very simple. I would have tried to draw a little attention to myself. I would have said: "I am hungry, I am dying, I am cold, I am in pain," or something. But she gave me much more—she gave me her grateful love. And she died with a smile on her face. Then there was the man we picked up from the drain, half eaten by worms, and after we had brought him to the home, he only said:

"I have lived like an animal in the street, but I am going to die as an angel, loved and cared for."

Then, after we had removed the worms from his body, all he said, with a big smile, was: "Sister, I am going home to God"—and he died. It was so wonderful to see the greatness of that man who could speak like that without blaming anybody, without comparing anything. Like an angel—this greatness of people who are spiritually rich even when they are materially poor. We are not social workers. We may be doing social work in the eyes of some people, but we must be contemplatives in the heart of the world. For we are touching the body of Christ and we are always in His presence.

You, too, must bring that presence of God into your family, for the family that prays together stays together.

There is so much hatred, so much misery, and we with our prayer, with our sacrifice, are beginning at home. Love begins at home, and it is not how much we do, but how much love we put into what we do.

If we are contemplatives in the heart of the world with all its problems, these problems can never discourage us. We must always remember what God tells us in Scripture: "Even if a mother could forget the child in her womb—something impossible, but even if she could forget—I will never forget you."

And so here I am talking with you. I want you to find the poor here, right in your own home first. And begin love there. Be that good news to your own people first. And find out about your next-door neighbors. Do you know who they are?

I had the most extraordinary experience of love of neighbor with a Hindu family. A gentleman came to our house and said: "Mother Teresa, there is a family who have not eaten for so long. Do something." So I took some rice and went there immediately. And I saw the children—their eyes shining with hunger. I don't know if you have ever seen hunger. But I have seen it very often. And the mother of the family took the rice I gave her and went out. When she came back, I asked her: "Where did you go? What did you do?" And she gave me a very simple answer: "They are hungry also." What struck me was that she knew—and who are they? A Muslim family—and she knew. I didn't bring any more rice that evening, because I wanted them, Hindus and Muslims, to enjoy the joy of sharing.

But there were those children, radiating joy, sharing the joy and peace with their mother because she had the love to give until it hurts. And you see this is where love begins—at home in the family.

So as the example of this family shows, God will never forget us, and there is something you and I can always do. We can keep the joy of loving Jesus in our hearts, and share that joy with all we come in contact with.

Let us make that one point—that no child will be unwanted, unloved, uncared for, or killed and thrown away. And give until it hurts—with a smile.

Because I talk so much of giving with a smile, once a professor from the United States asked me: "Are you married?" And I said: "Yes, and I find it sometimes very difficult to smile at my spouse, Jesus, because He can be very demanding—sometimes." This is really something true.

And there is where love comes in—when it is demanding, and yet we can give it with joy.

One of the most demanding things for me is traveling everywhere—and with publicity. I have said to Jesus that if I don't go to heaven for anything else, I will be going to heaven for all the traveling with all the publicity, because it has purified me and sacrificed me and made me really ready to go to heaven.

If we remember that God loves us, and that we can love others as He loves us, then America can become a sign of peace for the world.

From here, a sign of care for the weakest of the weak—the unborn child—must go out to the world. If you become a burning light of justice and peace in the world, then really you will be true to what the founders of this country stood for. God bless you!

Used by permission.

9

Billy Graham

THE WORLD'S DARKEST HOUR

=========

Billy Graham (1918–) has preached the gospel of Christ in person to more than eighty million people and to countless millions more over the airwaves and in videos. Nearly three million have responded to the invitation he offers at the end of his sermons. The ministry of the Billy Graham Evangelistic Association continues today. The following sermon was delivered October 18, 1958, during the Charlotte, North Carolina, crusade.

Now Matthew, the twenty-sixth chapter, beginning at the thirty-sixth verse: "Then cometh Jesus with them unto a place called Gethsemane, and saith unto the disciples, Sit ye here, while I go and pray yonder. And he took with him Peter and the two sons of Zebedee, and began to be sorrowful and very heavy. Then saith he unto them, My soul is exceeding sorrowful, even unto death: tarry ye here, and watch with me. And he went a little further, and fell on his face, and prayed, saying, O my Father, if it be possible, let this cup pass from me: nevertheless, not as I will, but as thou wilt" [verses 36–39 KJV].

I want you to see this picture tonight because the last twenty-four hours in the life of Christ was the darkest period in the history of the entire world. Here we find an incident in the last hours of the life of Christ which I want us to think about tonight and see what practical application we have in our own lives and the world in which we live.

Many people write to me and say, "We do not understand the gospel. We do not understand what you mean by receiving Christ or being born again." But I think more people write to me and say this:

They do not understand why Christ had to die on the cross in order for us to be saved. They do not understand the dark hours of Gethsemane. They do not understand why Christ voluntarily laid down His life. They do not understand why He endured the shame of the Cross. They do not understand all the phrases in the Bible that talk about the blood.

Many times in the Scriptures you find the phrase, "the blood of Christ" [Hebrews 9:14 KJV]; "the blood of Christ . . . cleanseth us from all sin" [see 1 John 1:7]. People revolt against that. They do not like that, and they wonder why that is in the Bible. They wonder why so much stress is placed upon the crucifixion and the resurrection of Jesus Christ. Tonight I want us to see that these last twenty-four hours in the life of Christ were the darkest in history, yet it was the darkness just before the dawn.

I believe that history repeats itself. And when the world comes to that moment of despair—that moment when it is about to blow itself apart, that moment when it seems there is no solution—at that moment, the sun will rise. The kingdom of God shall come because we have the promise in the Scripture that Jesus Christ, the Son of the living God, is coming back to this earth again. He is going to set up His kingdom, and then shall the prayer be answered as He taught in the Lord's Prayer, "Thy kingdom come" [Matthew 6:10 KJV]. His kingdom shall rule.

But before the triumph, before the crown, before the kingdom, before the victory, there had to come the suffering. Before you can share in Christ's victory, before you can have a new life here and now, before you can go to heaven, before you can claim the promise that we shall someday reign with Christ, you, too, must come to that same cross. You, too, must come in simple faith and stand at the foot of that cross and receive the Savior who was willing to go to the cross.

I want you to see Him on this night before He died. He has had the Last Supper with the disciples in the upper room, and they have gone now to the Mount of Olives. Now they are in the garden that is called Gethsemane. And Jesus leaves eight of His disciples on the out-skirts of the garden, and He takes three with Him—Peter, James, and John. He goes a little farther into the garden, and He tells these three disciples to watch and pray. Then He goes about a stone's throw far-ther along and falls prostrate on the ground and begins the agonizing prayer. Before He was finished, the Bible says He sweat, as it were, great drops of blood [see Luke 22:44].

What agony! How Christ must have prayed that night. Many times in Scripture you find Christ praying all night. If Jesus Christ had to pray all night, what about us in 1958? With our race problems, with our problem of communism, with the problem of crime that is getting worse with every passing day, with all the social problems that we face in the world and the personal problems and the problem of sin, we Americans are not praying. We are not calling upon God. We give lip service to God, but our hearts are far from Him [see Matthew 15:8].

Why, when the president of the United States gave a proclama-tion for a day of prayer the other day, you did not read very much about it. Very few churches observed it. Very few people spent any time in prayer. When the president said we should call on God, the people did not call on God.

We cannot call ourselves a Christian nation tonight. There are

Christians living in America, and Christian influences have been felt in this country; but we today are a heathen, pagan country. We are away from God. We have beautiful churches, but our hearts are far from God. We are not spending time in prayer. The blackest hour in history since the last twenty-four hours of the life of Christ we are living in today. We are living on the brink of hell itself, living on the brink of annihilation. And we are not praying. We are not calling upon God.

Jesus prayed and agonized until blood drops came out from Him. That night Jesus prayed a mysterious prayer, an unusual prayer, a strange prayer. He said, "O God, if it be possible, let this cup pass from Me. Nevertheless, not My will, but Thine, be done." What did He mean by that prayer, "Let this cup pass from Me"?

A cup of medicine is offered to a child, and he shrinks back. Then, at the bidding of his father, he takes it. That night a bitter cup was offered to Jesus, and He shrank from it. Why? I want you to see it tonight. Always the cross had been before Christ since the day He was at His baptism [see John 1:29]; at the temptation [see Matthew 4:1–11]; and at the marriage of Cana when He said, "My hour is not yet come" [see John 2:1–4]; when the crowd wanted to make Him a king at the Mount of Transfiguration, when He talked to Elijah and Moses [see Matthew 17:1–4]. He knew that He must die.

He told His disciples He must go to the cross. He read in the Old Testament Scriptures about the suffering the Messiah must endure. The shadow of the cross was before Him all the time. He knew that He had to go to the cross to pay for our sins if we were to be saved. But here was the final hour, and the cup of suffering was bitter.

In order for us to understand the chemical formula of the elixir of the cup that night, I want us to look into it deeply for a moment. I want us to see it and analyze it. I want us to see how much Christ endured that we might be forgiven of sin, that we might go to heaven, that we might have some hope of the solution of our problems.

The first element in that cup was physical pain. Men had died terrible deaths before. Men had been thrown into boiling water; men had been burned at the stake. Other men had died and suffered physical pain. But the death of the cross was something even worse than that. The death of the cross is said to be the worst possible torture that a man can endure. Because, first, they would strip a man to the waist. Then they would tie his hands together and bend him over and take long leather thongs with lead pellets or steel pellets embedded in the leather thongs, and beat him across the back until his back was in ribbons. And many times the lash of those thongs would come around his face and take his eyes out by the sockets, even tear his teeth out. Often death followed just the scourging and the floggings that were given by great, muscular men. Jesus endured that kind of flogging for you and for me.

Then they took a crown of thorns and placed it on His brow, and His face bled as they jerked His beard off. Then they spat in His face until He was covered from head to foot with the spittle of the people. Hatred, prejudice, intolerance, bigotry, all that the human heart could devise against Christ. Christ was not killed by Rome or Israel. The Bible tells us that Christ was crucified by you and me; my sins and your sins crucified Christ. We had a part in it, all the hatred of mankind.

We have seen in the past few days what hatred can do. We have seen how some men with sticks of dynamite can blow up synagogues just to express their hate. May God have mercy upon them. The human heart is expressed in that cross as they flogged Him, as they beat Him, as they spit on Him, as they put a crown of thorns on Him.

Then they gave Him a 250-pound cross to carry. He stumbled along the road with that cross until Simon of Cyrene had to come and help Him carry the cross [see Mark 15:21]. And I am certain Simon, today in heaven, is thrilled and proud of the fact that he helped Jesus carry the cross. Have you helped Jesus to carry the cross, or were you one of those putting nails in His hands?

You say, "But, Billy, I would never put a nail in Jesus' hands. I would never flog Him." Wouldn't you? You did it today! The sin that you committed today helped to crucify Christ because those people were all representative. We were expressing ourselves in them. You and I helped crucify Jesus. He was dying for our sins.

Then they took Him to Golgotha's mountain, and they put spikes in His hands. They tore His hands. They tore His hands and His feet. He never uttered a sound. The pain, the thirst—His tongue was swollen double. He hung hour upon hour on that terrible cross. Then at the end—many times when a person is dying on a cross, the ravenous birds, the vultures, would come with their ironlike beaks and pick at him while he was still alive. That was the cross.

And night—the night before He died, Jesus was on His knees before God and saying, "O God, if it is possible to save Billy Graham, if it is possible to save Jim Jones, if it is possible to save men and women some other way without Me having to endure that pain, O God, find it."

But there was another suffering. There was the suffering of loneliness, because Jesus went to the cross alone. No one else could go with Him. He was the Son of God. He was the only one in the universe who could bear all of our sins. He was the Paschal Lamb that Passover season, and the lamb had to be without blemish [see Exodus 12:5]. He was the Paschal Lamb being slain from the foundation of the world for our sins [see Revelation 13:8]. He alone had in His body and His soul the capacity to bear our sins.

Because, you see, we had sinned against God. We had rebelled against God, and we deserve death and we deserve judgment and we deserve hell. But Jesus said, "I will take the judgment, I will take the hell, and I will take the suffering." And He went to that cross alone because only He could suffer. Only He could be offered as a sacrifice that would be pleasing to God and would reconcile God and man together. So He endured it alone.

Judas was betraying Him for thirty pieces of silver, about twenty-one dollars [see Matthew 26:14–16]. You have betrayed Him today. The lie you told betrayed Jesus, the lustful thoughts that you have, the immoral deed that you did, the cheating that you did in business. How many times we have betrayed Him! We were a part of that betrayal and are just as guilty as Judas. And we will go to the same place as Judas went unless we repent of our sins and come to Jesus Christ and ask Him to forgive us.

Jesus died alone. The disciples forsook Him, and Peter denied Him. There He is, alone and hanging on the cross for our sins.

There are many types of loneliness. There is the loneliness of solitude. You have been alone when all you could hear was the thunder of the surf alongside the ocean on some faraway beach. I stood on a lonely beach in India, and I did not see a person for miles. The most beautiful beaches in the world, I think, are along the coral strands of India. I heard only the beating against the surf, against the rocks. Loneliness.

Admiral Byrd wrote in his book how he spent five months in the loneliness and darkness of the South Pole. Louis Zamperini, a friend of ours in California, spent thirty-five days alone on a life raft in loneliness, not knowing at any moment when he might be pulled down by a shark or when a Japanese plane would come and machine-gun him. Loneliness.

There are other types of loneliness. There is the loneliness of society. There is the poor creature who is living in a tenement house in New York tonight watching this telecast. You never receive a letter. You never hear a word of encouragement. You never know the handclasp of a friend. Or there is the wealthy society leader whose money has bought everything but happiness and joy. Or there is the country girl in New York or Los Angeles tonight who is seeking fame and fortune in the big city and has been disillusioned and disappointed, and now she is lonely. There is loneliness in a crowd, and some of you living in the midst of the big city are very lonely tonight. There is an emptiness in your heart.

I want to tell you something. You give your life to Christ tonight and He can become your friend, even closer than a brother [see Proverbs 18:24]. He can be with you in your loneliness.

Then there is the loneliness of suffering. Some of you are watching from hospital beds right now, from hospitals all over the country; and you are lonely lying there. A lady gave her life to Christ some time ago. And she said, "I've been crippled for five years with arthritis, and I have suffered. What a terrible suffering I have had." Then she added, "I have spent many a day alone, but never a lonely day."

Give your life to Christ, and you need never have a lonely day. Because, you see, Jesus has also suffered. He knows what it means to suffer, and in suffering He understands your suffering. He can come and put His hand on your brow and comfort you, and be there by your side during those lonely hours of suffering.

Then there is the loneliness of sorrow. You have been in the sickroom and you have seen a loved one snatched from you. You could not do anything about it. Your heart has been crushed by sorrow.

There is disappointment in your life. Maybe your husband has walked out on you. Maybe your boyfriend has left you, and your heart is crushed.

Jesus also suffered, and He knows. He stood at the grave of His friend Lazarus and wept [see John 11:35]. He knows what it means to have a crushing sorrow. He can be there with you right now. He can wipe those tears away. He can give you a joy and peace in your heart and take away that loneliness.

Then there is the loneliness of character. A man may find himself in a community or a society where he has to take a stand alone on some moral issue. It is not easy to stand alone. Moses had to stand alone [see Exodus 3:13–22]. Elijah on Mount Carmel had to stand alone. Everybody in the country was against Elijah. He was the only man that stood for God [see 1 Kings 18:17–46].

The fact is, we who know the Lord Jesus Christ as our Savior are in a small minority in the world. We are going to be standing more and more alone. Someday we may have to pay with our blood and our life for our faith in Jesus Christ. You are standing alone in your office. You are the only one who is trying to live for Christ on the high school campus. You are the only one in your class. You are the only one in your community trying to live for God. Sometimes you get discouraged and you feel lonely. Well, remember that almost everybody whom God ever used knew those hours of loneliness.

Then there is the loneliness of sin. That is the worst of all. The Bible says when Judas betrayed Jesus on that last night at the supper, he left the meeting of the disciples and he went out—because it was night [see John 13:30]. You remember when you were young and your conscience was sensitive. If you told a lie, your conscience spoke to you. But now it has become hardened and seared. There are many of you sitting at a bar right now. You wish your life were different. You wish that you were not chained by the habits of sin tonight. You would like to be through but you cannot, although you have tried. Yes, there is loneliness of sin. The older you get the more lonely you will be, because you will be farther away from God. There is nothing but loneliness and remorse.

Go ahead and continue for a while. The Bible says there is pleasure in sin for a season [see Hebrews 11:25]. You can get away with it for a while.

A man told me one day, "I'm not afraid of going to hell; there are going to be a lot of other people down there." But, listen, the Bible indicates that hell is a lonely place. You won't see anybody else there. You won't even see the devil. A lot of people have an idea that hell is a place where the devil is standing at a furnace and giving the orders, or sitting in a big office running hell. That is not the picture at all.

The picture is one of separation from God and the blackness of night, darkness and loneliness. You will be all alone. You won't see your husband or your wife. You won't see your friends. You will be alone— the loneliness of sin. Sin pays wages [see Romans 6:23]. And it crushes your personality, it crushes your life, it crushes your soul, and it ends up in hell.

Turn to Christ tonight from your sins. Let Him free you. Let Christ come in, and then heaven will be a place of fellowship with your loved ones. Heaven will be a glorious world of fellowship and friendship. There will be no loneliness in heaven. The Bible says there will be no night there [see Revelation 22:5]. What a hope we have, those of us who know Jesus Christ as our Savior.

The Bible says Christ suffered alone. "I have trodden the winepress alone; and of the people there was none with me" [Isaiah 63:3 KJV], said Jesus.

The third element in this bitter cup was the mental anguish. Jesus had quoted Isaiah the prophet. Jesus knew He had to suffer. He knew something about the affliction of the next day and that night in the garden. He knew what was going to take place, and naturally He was suffering much anguish as He thought about the suffering of the next day.

We have thousands of people in America who are suffering mentally. We have thousands of psychological problems. We have thousands of people in our mental institutions. We have thousands of people today who are confused mentally. I want to tell you that Jesus can touch your mind if you will let Him come in. Because thousands of our mental problems are the result of spiritual separation from God, or they are the result of idolatry. They are the result of putting other things before God, and that causes mental unbalance many times. There are thousands of people who are suffering mentally.

Down here in the South, there are thousands of people who are suffering anguish at this particular time. It is not just a Southern problem. It is a world problem. It is the problem on Cyprus; it is the problem in the Middle East; it is the problem in New York; it is the problem in Chicago; it is the problem in the Far East; it is the problem in India. Thousands of people are searching their souls. Their minds are tortured and bewildered, wondering what is the right thing to do in such a complicated situation.

I tell you Christ is the answer. Come to Christ. Come to the foot of the cross and let Him touch your mind, and your heart, and relax your soul. Then shall we have love for our fellow man, as love knows no bounds, and we shall love our neighbors as ourselves [see Matthew 19:19].

There are thousands of people who want to obey the law, but they don't know what the law is. The federal government says one thing and the state government says another, and they are confused. The tremendous confusion comes because it is a constitutional problem as well as a race problem. Many people are making emotional statements at the moment, flag-waving statements, hysterical statements. Would to God that all of us could come to the cross and see in Christ a solution to all the problems that bewilder us and confuse us.

That may not be your problem. There may be some other problem in your life, but you need Jesus. You need Christ. The country needs Christ.

The fourth element in this bitter cup that Jesus was about to drink was the cup of the anguish of soul. The physical pain, the loneliness of its shame, and the mental anguish were nothing compared to the spiritual suffering which Jesus Christ suffered on the cross that day. That night He was thinking about God, and His suffering was wrapped up in one little word—*sin*. Because that next day Jesus was going to become guilty of your sins and my sins. A cloud was going to pass between Him and God—a cloud, for the first time—and His pure, righteous soul was going to be filled with sin. Your sins were going to be laid on Him. The Scripture says that God had "laid on him the iniquity of us all" [Isaiah 53:6 KJV]. The Bible says He was "made . . . to be sin for us, who knew no sin" [2 Corinthians 5:21 KJV]. He had never known sin, but He was made to be sin.

His soul must have shuddered. His soul must have been shaken. How Jesus must have looked with horror. He said, "O God, if it is possible, let this cup pass from Me. O God, I don't want to have to drink this cup. If there is any other way to save men, if there is any other way for the world to be saved, let it be done."

But the Bible says you cannot work for it. The Bible says, "By grace are ye saved through faith; and that not of yourselves: it is the gift of God: not of works, lest any man should boast" [Ephesians 2:8–9 KJV]. You can work your fingers to the bone doing good work, but that will not save your soul. You are not saved by works. Suppose a man could pay for it. Suppose you had a billion dollars tonight, suppose you were the richest man in the world, and you gave it all to charity, and you gave it all to God. Would you go to heaven? Not unless you had come to the cross. Because, you see, if you could have bought your way, or if you could have worked your way, or if you could have schemed your way to heaven, Jesus need never have gone to the cross. That night God would have said, "Jesus, You do not have to go to the cross." But God did not say that to His Son. There was no other way.

If I could tell you another way of salvation that is easier, I would tell you. I tell you tonight after studying this book for twenty years, there is no other name given among men whereby we must be saved except the name of Jesus [see Acts 4:12]. There is no other way of salvation except at the foot of the cross.

When I look at the cross tonight, I see four things. I see, first, the terribleness of sins. I know that I am a sinner. When I look at Christ dying in my place on the cross and realize the things that I have done and that it was my sins that nailed Him there, I must cry out to God, "O God, I am a sinner."

The second thing I see is the amazing love of God, that "God commendeth his love toward us, in that, while we were yet sinners, Christ died for us" [Romans 5:8 KJV]. You have rebelled against God; you have sinned against God; you have done things that you know you should not have done. You have helped even crucify Jesus. But in spite of it, God loves you. And on the cross there is written in gigantic letters in neon fire, "God so loved the world, that he gave his only begotten Son, that whosoever believeth in him should not perish, but have everlasting life" [John 3:16 KJV]. There is the love of God. And if you have any doubt concerning the love of God, look at the cross. It was there that He died for us.

Third, in that cross I find my complete redemption. Christ bowed His head and said, "It is finished" [John 19:30 KJV]. I cannot add anything to it. I cannot take anything away. If I am ever to get to heaven, I will have to come to the cross. If I am ever to have my sins forgiven, I will have to come to the cross.

I want to ask you tonight, have you ever been to the cross? Are you sure that you have had this encounter with God at the cross? You may be a member of the church. You may live a moral life. You may be a decent person. I don't know who you are or what you are. It doesn't make any difference where you come from or what your nationality background is, what state you live in, how rich or how poor, how educated or uneducated; you have to come to the cross. Jesus said it's a narrow gate, and the gate is the cross.

If you are not sure that you have been there, renouncing your sin and receiving Christ, you come tonight. Because I do not see how any person can resist the love of God. Many people ask me what is the unpardonable sin. I tell you it is the sin that God cannot pardon. Any man or woman that rejects or resists His Son, Jesus Christ—that's the unpardonable sin. "There remaineth no more sacrifice for sins" [Hebrews 10:26 KJV]. There is no other way. I tell you, my beloved friends of this great nation, there is only one way of forgiveness and redemption and salvation, and that is the cross of Christ.

I am asking you to come to the cross tonight. I am asking you to come by faith and say, "O God, I have sinned. O God, I am sorry for the things I have done. I am coming by faith to receive Thy Son, Jesus Christ." Don't neglect it. Don't put it off until another night. You may never have another moment quite like this tonight.

God says, "I want to meet you. I want to help you. But I'll only meet you and help you at one place, and that is at the cross." It may look foolish for me to say, "Get up out of your seat and come." Don't ask me how it happens. I only know that when a man comes to Christ, he can never be the same again. I only know that his life is changed if he comes to the cross. And I am going to ask you to come right now.

Reprinted with permission of the Billy Graham Evangelistic Association; brackets in original.

10

Jonathan Edwards

SINNERS IN THE HANDS OF AN ANGRY GOD

———

Jonathan Edwards (1703–1758), a colonial New England minister and missionary, was one of the greatest preachers and theologians in American history. Ingeniously, he used the science of John Locke and Isaac Newton to reshape man's understanding of God.

> *Their foot shall slide in due time.*
> —Deuteronomy 32:35 KJV

In this verse is threatened the vengeance of God on the wicked unbelieving Israelites, who were God's visible people, and who lived under the means of grace; but who, notwithstanding all God's wonderful works towards them, remained (as verse 28) void of counsel, having no understanding in them. Under all the cultivations of heaven, they brought forth bitter and poisonous fruit; as in the two verses next preceding the text. The expression I have chosen for my text, "Their foot shall slide in due time," seems to imply the following doings, relating to the punishment and destruction to which these wicked Israelites were exposed.

1. That they were always exposed to *destruction*; as one that stands or walks in slippery places is always exposed to fall. This is implied in the manner of their destruction coming upon them, being represented by their foot sliding. The same is expressed in Psalm 73:18: "Surely thou didst set them in slippery places; thou castedst them down into destruction."

2. It implies that they were always exposed to sudden unexpected destruction. As he that walks in slippery places is every moment liable to fall, he cannot foresee one moment whether he shall stand or fall the next; and when he does fall, he falls at once without warning, which is also expressed in Psalm 73:18–19: "Surely thou didst set them in slippery places; thou castedst them down into destruction. How are they brought into desolation, as in a moment!" [KJV].

3. Another thing implied is that they are liable to fall *of themselves*, without being thrown down by the hand of another; as he that stands or walks on slippery ground needs nothing but his own weight to throw him down.

4. That the reason why they are not fallen already, and do not fall now, is only that God's appointed time is not come. For it is said that when that due time, or appointed time, comes, *their foot shall slide*. Then they shall be left to fall, as they are inclined by their own weight. God will not hold them up in these slippery places any longer, but will let them go; and then at that very instant, they shall fall into destruction; as he that stands on such slippery declining ground, on the edge of a pit, he cannot stand alone; when he is let go, he immediately falls and is lost.

The observation from the words that I would now insist upon is this: "There is nothing that keeps wicked men at any one moment out of hell, but the mere pleasure of God." By the mere pleasure of God, I mean His sovereign pleasure, His arbitrary will, restrained by no obligation, hindered by no manner of difficulty, any more than if nothing else but God's mere will had in the least degree, or in any respect whatsoever, any hand in the preservation of wicked men one moment.

The truth of this observation may appear by the following considerations.

1. There is no want of *power* in God to cast wicked men into hell at any moment. Men's hands cannot be strong when God rises up. The strongest have no power to resist Him, nor can any deliver out of His hands. He is not only able to cast wicked men into hell, but He can most easily do it. Sometimes an earthly prince meets with a great deal of difficulty to subdue a rebel, who has found means to fortify himself, and has made himself strong by the numbers of his followers. But it is not so with God. There is no fortress that is any defense from the power of God. Though hand join in hand, and vast multitudes of God's enemies combine and associate themselves, they are easily broken in pieces. They are as great heaps of light chaff before the whirlwind; or large quantities of dry stubble before devouring flames. We find it easy to tread on and crush a worm that we see crawling on the earth; so it is easy for us to cut or singe a slender thread that anything hangs by: thus easy is it for God, when He pleases, to cast His enemies down to hell. What are we, that we should think to stand before Him, at whose rebuke the earth trembles, and before whom the rocks are thrown down?

2. They *deserve* to be cast into hell; so that divine justice never stands in the way, it makes no objection against God's using His power at any moment to destroy them. Yea, on the contrary, justice calls aloud for an infinite punishment of their sins. Divine justice says of the tree that brings forth such grapes of Sodom, "Cut it down; why cumbereth it the ground?" (Luke 13:7 KJV). The sword of divine justice is every moment brandished over their heads, and it is nothing but the hand of arbitrary mercy, and God's mere will, that holds it back.

3. They are already under a sentence of *condemnation* to hell. They

do not only justly deserve to be cast down thither, but the sentence of the law of God, that eternal and immutable rule of righteousness that God has fixed between Him and mankind, is gone out against them, and stands against them; so that they are bound over already to hell: "He that believeth not is condemned already" (John 3:18 KJV). So that every unconverted man properly belongs to hell; that is his place; from thence he is, (John 8:23 KJV). "Ye are from beneath." And thither he is bound; it is the place that justice, and God's word, and the sentence of his unchangeable law assign to him.

4. They are now the objects of that very same anger and wrath of God that is expressed in the torments of hell. And the reason why they do not go down to hell at each moment is not because God, in whose power they are, is not then very angry with them; as He is with many miserable creatures now tormented in hell, who there feel and bear the fierceness of His wrath. Yea, God is a great deal more angry with great numbers that are now on earth: yea, doubtless, with many that are now in this congregation, who it may be are at ease, than He is with many of those who are now in the flames of hell.

So that it is not because God is unmindful of their wickedness, and does not resent it, that He does not let loose His hand and cut them off. God is not altogether such a one as themselves, though they may imagine Him to be so. The wrath of God burns against them, their damnation does not slumber; the pit is prepared, the fire is made ready, the furnace is now hot, ready to receive them; the flames do now rage and glow. The glittering sword is whet, and held over them, and the pit hath opened its mouth under them.

5. The *devil* stands ready to fall upon them, and seize them as his own, at what moment God shall permit him. They belong to him; he has their souls in his possession, and under his dominion. The Scripture represents them as his "goods", (Luke 11:21). The devils watch them; they are ever by them at their right hand; they stand waiting for them,

like greedy, hungry lions that see their prey, and expect to have it, but are for the present kept back. If God should withdraw His hand, by which they are restrained, they would in one moment fly upon their poor souls. The old serpent is gaping for them; hell opens its mouth wide to receive them; and if God should permit it, they would be hastily swallowed up and lost.

6. There are in the souls of wicked men those hellish principles reigning that would presently kindle and flame out into hellfire, if it were not for God's restraints. There is laid in the very nature of carnal men a foundation for the torments of hell. There are those corrupt principles, in reigning power in them, and in full possession of them, that are seeds of hellfire. These principles are active and powerful, exceeding violent in their nature, and if it were not for the restraining hand of God upon them, they would soon break out, they would flame out after the same manner as the same corruptions, the same enmity does in the hearts of damned souls, and would beget the same torments as they do in them. The souls of the wicked are in Scripture compared to the troubled sea (Isaiah 57:20). For the present, God restrains their wickedness by His mighty power, as He does the raging waves of the troubled sea, saying, "Hitherto shalt thou come, but no further"; but if God should withdraw that restraining power, it would soon carry all before it. Sin is the ruin and misery of the soul; it is destructive in its nature; and if God should leave it without restraint, there would need nothing else to make the soul perfectly miserable. The corruption of the heart of man is immoderate and boundless in its fury; and while wicked men live here, it is like fire pent up by God's restraints, whereas if it were let loose, it would set on fire the course of nature; and as the heart is now a sink of sin, so if sin was not restrained, it would immediately turn the soul into a fiery oven, or a furnace of fire and brimstone.

7. It is no security to wicked men for one moment that there are

no visible means of death at hand. It is no security to a natural man that he is now in health, and that he does not see which way he should now immediately go out of the world by any accident, and that there is no visible danger in any respect in his circumstances. The manifold and continual experience of the world in all ages shows this is no evidence that a man is not on the very brink of eternity, and that the next step will not be into another world. The unseen, unthought-of ways and means of persons going suddenly out of the world are innumerable and inconceivable. Unconverted men walk over the pit of hell on a rotten covering, and there are innumerable places in this covering so weak that they will not bear their weight, and these places are not seen. The arrows of death fly unseen at noonday; the sharpest sight cannot discern them. God has so many different unsearchable ways of taking wicked men out of the world and sending them to hell that there is nothing to make it appear that God had need to be at the expense of a miracle, or go out of the ordinary course of His providence, to destroy any wicked man, at any moment. All the means that there are of sinners going out of the world are so in God's hands, and so universally and absolutely subject to His power and determination, that it does not depend at all the less on the mere will of God, whether sinners shall at any moment go to hell, than if means were never made use of or at all concerned in the case.

8. Natural men's prudence and care to preserve their own lives, or the care of others to preserve them, do not secure them a moment. To this, divine providence and universal experience do also bear testimony. There is this clear evidence that men's own wisdom is no security to them from death; that if it were otherwise, we should see some difference between the wise and politic men of the world and others, with regard to their liableness to early and unexpected death; but how is it in fact? "How dieth the wise man? as the fool" (Ecclesiastes 2:16 KJV).

9. All wicked men's pains and contrivance which they use to escape hell, while they continue to reject Christ, and so remain wicked men, do not secure them from hell one moment. Almost every natural man that hears of hell flatters himself that he shall escape it; he depends upon himself for his own security; he flatters himself in what he has done, in what he is now doing, or what he intends to do. Everyone lays out matters in his own mind how he shall avoid damnation, and flatters himself that he contrives well for himself and that his schemes will not fail. They hear indeed that there are but few saved, and that the greater part of men that have died heretofore are gone to hell; but each one imagines that he lays out matters better for his own escape than others have done. He does not intend to come to that place of torment; he says within himself, that he intends to take effectual care, and to order matters so for himself as not to fail.

But the foolish children of men miserably delude themselves in their own schemes, and in confidence in their own strength and wisdom; they trust to nothing but a shadow. The greater part of those who heretofore have lived under the same means of grace, and are now dead, are undoubtedly gone to hell; and it was not because they were not as wise as those who are now alive: it was not because they did not lay out matters as well for themselves to secure their own escape. If we could speak with them, and inquire of them, one by one, whether they expected, when alive, and when they used to hear about hell, ever to be the subjects of that misery, we doubtless should hear one and another reply, "No, I never intended to come here. I had laid out matters otherwise in my mind; I thought I should contrive well for myself; I thought my scheme good. I intended to take effectual care; but it came upon me unexpected. I did not look for it at that time, and in that manner; it came as a thief. Death outwitted me. God's wrath was too quick for me. Oh, my cursed foolishness! I was flattering myself, and pleasing myself with vain dreams of what I would do hereafter; and when I was saying, "Peace and safety," then suddenly destruction came upon me.

10. God has laid Himself under *no obligation* by any promise to keep any natural man out of hell one moment. God certainly has made no promises either of eternal life, or of any deliverance or preservation from eternal death, but what are contained in the covenant of grace, the promises that are given in Christ, in whom all the promises are yea and amen. But surely they have no interest in the promises of the covenant of grace who are not the children of the covenant, who do not believe in any of the promises, and have no interest in the Mediator of the covenant.

So that whatever some have imagined and pretended about promises made to natural men's earnest seeking and knocking, it is plain and manifest that whatever pains a natural man takes in religion, whatever prayers he makes, till he believes in Christ, God is under no manner of obligation to keep him a moment from eternal destruction.

So that thus it is that natural men are held in the hand of God, over the pit of hell; they have deserved the fiery pit, and are already sentenced to it; and God is dreadfully provoked. His anger is as great towards them as to those that are actually suffering the executions of the fierceness of His wrath in hell, and they have done nothing in the least to appease or abate that anger. Neither is God in the least bound by any promise to hold them up one moment. The devil is waiting for them, hell is gaping for them, the flames gather and flash about them, and would fain lay hold on them, and swallow them up; the fire pent up in their own hearts is struggling to break out; and they have no interest in any Mediator. There are no means within reach that can be any security to them. In short, they have no refuge, nothing to take hold of; all that preserves them every moment is the mere arbitrary will and uncovenanted, unobliged forbearance of an incensed God.

APPLICATION

The use of this awful subject may be for awakening unconverted persons in this congregation. This that you have heard is the case of every one of you that are out of Christ. That world of misery, that lake of burning brimstone, is extended abroad under you. There is the dreadful pit of the glowing flames of the wrath of God; there is hell's wide, gaping mouth open; and you have nothing to stand upon, nor anything to take hold of. There is nothing between you and hell but the air; it is only the power and mere pleasure of God that holds you up.

You probably are not sensible of this; you find you are kept out of hell, but do not see the hand of God in it; but look at other things, as the good state of your bodily constitution, your care of your own life, and the means you use for your own preservation. But indeed these things are nothing; if God should withdraw His hand, they would avail no more to keep you from falling than the thin air to hold up a person that is suspended in it.

Your wickedness makes you as it were heavy as lead, and to tend downwards with great weight and pressure towards hell; and if God should let you go, you would immediately sink and swiftly descend and plunge into the bottomless gulf, and your healthy constitution, and your own care and prudence, and best contrivance, and all your right-eousness, would have no more influence to uphold you and keep you out of hell than a spider's web would have to stop a falling rock. Were it not for the sovereign pleasure of God, the earth would not bear you one moment; for you are a burden to it; the creation groans with you; the creature is made subject to the bondage of your corruption, not willingly; the sun does not willingly shine upon you to give you light to serve sin and Satan; the earth does not willingly yield her increase to satisfy your lusts; nor is it willingly a stage for your wickedness to be acted upon; the air does not willingly serve you for breath to maintain the flame of life in your vitals, while you spend your life in the service of God's enemies. God's creatures are good, and were made for men to serve God with, and do not willingly subserve to any other purpose, and groan when they are abused to purposes so directly contrary to their nature and end. And the world would spew you out, were it not for the sovereign hand of Him who hath subjected it in hope. There are black clouds of God's wrath now hanging directly over your heads, full of the dreadful storm, and big with thunder; and were it not for the restraining hand of God, it would immediately burst forth upon you. The sovereign pleasure of God, for the present, stays His rough wind; otherwise it would come with fury, and your destruction would come like a whirlwind, and you would be like the chaff of the summer threshing floor.

The wrath of God is like great waters that are dammed for the present; they increase more and more, and rise higher and higher, till an outlet is given; and the longer the stream is stopped, the more rapid and mighty is its course, when once it is let loose. It is true that judgment against your evil works has not been executed hitherto; the floods of God's vengeance have been withheld; but your guilt in the meantime is constantly increasing, and you are every day treasuring up more wrath; the waters are constantly rising, and waxing more and more mighty; and there is nothing but the mere pleasure of God that holds the waters back, that are unwilling to be stopped, and press hard to go forward. If God should only withdraw His hand from the floodgate, it would immediately fly open, and the fiery floods of the fierceness and wrath of God would rush forth with inconceivable fury, and would come upon you with omnipotent power; and if your strength were ten thousand times greater than it is, yea, ten thousand times greater than the strength of the stoutest, sturdiest devil in hell, it would be nothing to withstand or endure it.

The bow of God's wrath is bent, and the arrow made ready on the string, and justice bends the arrow at your heart, and strains the bow; and it is nothing but the mere pleasure of God, and that of an angry God, without any promise or obligation at all, that keeps the arrow one moment from being made drunk with your blood. Thus all you that never passed under a great change of heart, by the mighty power of the Spirit of God upon your souls; all you that were never born again, and made new creatures, and raised from being dead in sin to a state of new, and before altogether unexperienced light and life, are in the hands of an angry God. However you may have reformed your life in many things, and may have had religious affections, and may keep up a form of religion in your families and closets, and in the house of God, it is nothing but His mere pleasure that keeps you from being this moment swallowed up in everlasting destruction. However unconvinced you may now be of the truth of what you hear, by and by you will be fully convinced of it. Those that are gone from being in the like circumstances with you see that it was so with them; for destruction came suddenly upon most of them; when they expected nothing of it, and while they were saying, "Peace and safety" now they see that those things on which they depended for peace and safety were nothing but thin air and empty shadows.

The God that holds you over the pit of hell, much as one holds a spider, or some loathsome insect over the fire, abhors you, and is dreadfully provoked: His wrath towards you burns like fire; He looks upon you as worthy of nothing else but to be cast into the fire; He is of purer eyes than to bear to have you in His sight; you are ten thousand times more abominable in His eyes than the most hateful venomous serpent is in ours. You have offended Him infinitely more than ever a stubborn rebel did his prince; and yet it is nothing but His hand that holds you from falling into the fire every moment. It is to be ascribed to nothing else that you did not go to hell the last night; that you [were] suffered to awake again in this world after you closed your eyes to sleep. And there is no other reason to be given, why you have not dropped into hell since you arose in the morning, but that God's hand has held you up. There is no other reason to be given why you have not gone to hell since you have sat here in the house of God, provoking His pure eyes by your sinful wicked manner of attending His solemn worship. Yea, there is nothing else that is to be given as a reason why you do not this very moment drop down into hell.

O sinner! Consider the fearful danger you are in: it is a great furnace of wrath, a wide and bottomless pit, full of the fire of wrath, that you are held over in the hand of that God, whose wrath is provoked and incensed as much against you as against many of the damned in hell. You hang by a slender thread, with the flames of divine wrath flashing about it, and ready every moment to singe it, and burn it asunder; and you have no interest in any Mediator, and nothing to lay hold of to save yourself, nothing to keep off the flames of wrath, nothing of your own, nothing that you ever have done, nothing that you can do, to induce God to spare you one moment. And consider here more particularly several things concerning that wrath that you are in such danger of.

1. *Whose* wrath it is: it is the wrath of the infinite God. If it were only the wrath of man, though it were of the most potent prince, it would be comparatively little to be regarded. The wrath of kings is very much dreaded, especially of absolute monarchs, who have the possessions and lives of their subjects wholly in their power, to be disposed of at their mere will. "The fear of a king is as the roaring of a lion: whoso provoketh him to anger sinneth against his own soul" (Proverbs 20:2 KJV). The subject that very much enrages an arbitrary prince is liable to suffer the most extreme torments that human art can invent, or human power can inflict. But the greatest earthly potentates in their greatest majesty and strength, and when clothed in their greatest terrors, are but feeble, despicable worms of the dust, in comparison of the great and almighty Creator and King of heaven and earth. It is but little that they can do,

when most enraged, and when they have exerted the utmost of their fury. All the kings of the earth, before God, are as grasshoppers; they are nothing, and less than nothing: both their love and their hatred are to be despised. The wrath of the great King of kings is as much more terrible than theirs as His majesty is greater. "And I say unto you, my friends, Be not afraid of them that kill the body, and after that have no more that they can do. But I will forewarn you whom ye shall fear: Fear him, which after he hath killed hath power to cast into hell; yea, I say unto you, Fear him" (Luke 12:4–5 KJV).

2. It is the *fierceness* of His wrath that you are exposed to. We often read of the fury of God; as in Isaiah 59:18: "According to their deeds, accordingly he will repay fury to his adversaries." So Isaiah 66:15: "For, behold, the LORD will come with fire, and with his chariots like a whirlwind, to render his anger with fury, and his rebuke with flames of fire" [KJV]. And in many other places. So in Revelation 19:15, we read of "the winepress of the fierceness and wrath of Almighty God" [KJV]. The words are exceeding terrible. If it had only been said, "the wrath of God," the words would have implied that which is infinitely dreadful: but it is "the fierceness and wrath of God." The fury of God! The fierceness of Jehovah! Oh, how dreadful must that be! Who can utter or conceive what such expressions carry in them! But it is also "the fierceness and wrath of *Almighty* God." As though there would be a very great manifestation of His almighty power in what the fierceness of His wrath should inflict, as though omnipotence should be as it were enraged, and exerted, as men are wont to exert their strength in the fierceness of their wrath. Oh! then what will be the consequence! What will become of the poor worms that shall suffer it! Whose hands can be strong? And whose heart can endure? To what a dreadful, inexpressible, inconceivable depth of misery must the poor creature be sunk who shall be the subject of this!

Consider this, you that are here present, that yet remain in an unregenerate state. That God will execute the fierceness of His anger implies that He will inflict wrath without any pity. When God beholds the ineffable extremity of your case, and sees your torment to be so vastly disproportioned to your strength, and sees how your poor soul is crushed, and sinks down, as it were, into an infinite gloom, He will have no compassion upon you; He will not forbear the executions of His wrath, or in the least lighten His hand; there shall be no moderation or mercy, nor will God then at all stay His rough wind; He will have no regard to your welfare, nor be at all careful lest you should suffer too much in any other sense than only that you shall *not suffer beyond what strict justice requires*. Nothing shall be withheld because it is so hard for you to bear. "Therefore will I also deal in fury: mine eye shall not spare, neither will I have pity: and though they cry in mine ears with a loud voice, yet will I not hear them" (Ezekiel 8:18 KJV). Now God stands ready to pity you; this is a day of mercy; you may cry now with some encouragement of obtaining mercy. But when once the day of mercy is past, your most lamentable and dolorous cries and shrieks will be in vain; you will be wholly lost and thrown away of God, as to any regard to your welfare. God will have no other use to put you to but to suffer misery; you shall be continued in being to no other end; for you will be a vessel of wrath fitted to destruction; and there will be no other use of this vessel but to be filled full of wrath. God will be so far from pitying you when you cry to Him that it is said He will only "laugh and mock" (Proverbs 1:26 ff.).

How awful are those words, Isaiah 63:3, which are the words of the great God: "I will tread them in mine anger, and trample them in my fury; and their blood shall be sprinkled upon my garments, and I will stain all my raiment" [KJV]. It is perhaps impossible to conceive of words that carry in them greater manifestations of these three things, *vis.* contempt, and hatred, and fierceness of indignation. If you cry to God to pity you, He will be so far from pitying you in your doleful case, or showing you the least regard or favor, that instead of that, He will only tread you underfoot. And though He will know that you cannot bear the weight of omnipotence treading upon you, yet He will not regard that, but He will crush you under His feet without mercy; He will crush out your blood, and make it fly, and it shall be sprinkled on His garments, so as to stain all His raiment. He will not only hate you, but He will have you in the utmost contempt: no place shall be thought fit for you but under His feet to be trodden down as the mire of the streets.

The misery you are exposed to is that which God will inflict to that end, that He might show what that wrath of Jehovah is. God hath had it on His heart to show to angels and men both how excellent His love is, and also how terrible His wrath is. Sometimes earthly kings have a mind to show how terrible their wrath is by the extreme punishments they would execute on those that would provoke them. Nebuchadnezzar, that mighty and haughty monarch of the Chaldean Empire, was willing to show his wrath when enraged with Shadrach, Meshech, and Abednego; and accordingly gave orders that the burning fiery furnace should be heated seven times hotter than it was before; doubtless, it was raised to the utmost degree of fierceness that human art could raise it. But the great God is also willing to show His wrath, and magnify His awful majesty and mighty power in the extreme sufferings of His enemies. "What if God, willing to shew his wrath, and to make his power known, endured with much longsuffering the vessels of wrath fitted to destruction?" (Romans 9:22 KJV). And seeing this is His design, and what He has determined, even to show how terrible the unrestrained wrath, the fury and fierceness of Jehovah is, He will do it to effect. There will be something accomplished and brought to pass that will be dreadful with a witness. When the great and angry God hath risen up and executed His awful vengeance on the poor sinner, and the wretch is actually suffering the infinite weight and power of His indignation, then will God call upon the whole universe to behold that awful majesty and mighty power that is to be seen in it. "And the people shall be as the burnings of lime: as thorns cut up shall they be burned in the fire. Hear, ye that are far off, what I have done; and, ye that are near, acknowledge my might. The sinners in Zion are afraid; fearfulness hath surprised the hypocrites" (Isaiah 33:12–14 KJV).

Thus it will be with you that are in an unconverted state, if you continue in it; the infinite might, and majesty, and terribleness of the omnipotent God shall be magnified upon you, in the ineffable strength of your torments. You shall be tormented in the presence of the holy angels, and in the presence of the Lamb; and when you shall be in this state of suffering, the glorious inhabitants of heaven shall go forth and look on the awful spectacle, that they may see what the wrath and fierceness of the Almighty is; and when they have seen it, they will fall down and adore that great power and majesty. "And it shall come to pass, that from one new moon to another, and from one sabbath to another, shall all flesh come to worship before me, saith the LORD. And they shall go forth, and look upon the carcases of the men that have transgressed against me: for their worm shall not die, neither shall their fire be quenched; and they shall be an abhorring unto all flesh" (Isaiah 66:23–24 KJV).

4. It is *everlasting* wrath. It would be dreadful to suffer this fierceness and wrath of Almighty God one moment; but you must suffer it to all eternity. There will be no end to this exquisite horrible misery. When you look forward, you shall see a long forever, a boundless duration before you, which will swallow up your thoughts, and amaze your soul; and you will absolutely despair of ever having any deliverance, any end, any mitigation, any rest at all. You will know certainly that you must wear out long ages, millions of millions of ages, in wrestling and conflicting with this almighty merciless vengeance; and then when you have so done, when so many ages have actually been spent by you in this manner, you will know that all is but a point to what

remains. So that your punishment will indeed be infinite. Oh, who can express what the state of a soul in such circumstances is! All that we can possibly say about it gives but a very feeble, faint representation of it; it is inexpressible and inconceivable: For "who knows the power of God's anger?"

How dreadful is the state of those that are daily and hourly in the danger of this great wrath and infinite misery! But this is the dismal case of every soul in this congregation that has not been born again, however moral and strict, sober and religious, they may otherwise be. Oh, that you would consider it, whether you be young or old! There is reason to think that there are many in this congregation now hearing this discourse that will actually be the subjects of this very misery to all eternity. We know not who they are, or in what seats they sit, or what thoughts they now have. It may be they are now at ease, and hear all these things without much disturbance, and are now flattering themselves that they are not the persons, promising themselves that they shall escape. If we knew that there was one person, and but one, in the whole congregation that was to be the subject of this misery, what an awful thing would it be to think of! If we knew who it was, what an awful sight would it be to see such a person! How might all the rest of the congregation lift up a lamentable and bitter cry over him! But alas! Instead of one, how many is it likely will remember this discourse in hell? And it would be a wonder if some that are now present should not be in hell in a very short time, even before this year is out. And it would be no wonder if some persons that now sit here in some seats of this meeting house, in health, quiet, and secure, should be there before tomorrow morning. Those of you that finally continue in a natural condition, that shall keep out of hell longest, will be there in a little time! Your damnation does not slumber; it will come swiftly, and, in all probability, very suddenly upon many of you. You have reason to wonder that you are not already in hell. It is doubtless the case of some whom you have seen and known, that never deserved hell more than you, and that heretofore appeared as likely to have been now alive as you. Their case is past all hope; they are crying in extreme misery and perfect despair; but here you are in the land of the living and in the house of God, and have an opportunity to obtain salvation. What would not those poor damned hopeless souls give for one day's opportunity such as you now enjoy!

And now you have an extraordinary opportunity, a day wherein Christ has thrown the door of mercy wide open, and stands in calling and crying with a loud voice to poor sinners; a day wherein many are flocking to Him, and pressing into the kingdom of God. Many are daily coming from the east, west, north, and south; many that were very lately in the same miserable condition that you are in are now in a happy state, with their hearts filled with love to Him who has loved them, and washed them from their sins in His own blood, and rejoicing in hope of the glory of God. How awful is it to be left behind at such a day! To see so many others feasting, while you are pining and perishing! To see so many rejoicing and singing for joy of heart, while you have cause to mourn for sorrow of heart, and howl for vexation of spirit! How can you rest one moment in such a condition? Are not your souls as precious as the souls of the people at Suffield [a town in the neighborhood], where they are flocking from day to day to Christ?

Are there not many here who have lived long in the world, and are not to this day born again, and so are aliens from the commonwealth of Israel, and have done nothing ever since they have lived, but treasure up wrath against the day of wrath? Oh, sirs, your case, in an especial manner, is extremely dangerous. Your guilt and hardness of heart is extremely great. Do you not see how generally persons of your years are passed over and left, in the present remarkable and wonderful dispensation of God's mercy? You had need to consider yourselves, and awake thoroughly out of sleep. You cannot bear the fierceness and wrath of the infinite God. And you, young men, and young women, will you neglect this precious season which you now enjoy, when so many others of your age are renouncing all youthful vanities, and flocking to Christ? You especially have now an extraordinary opportunity; but if you neglect it, it will soon be with you as with those persons who spent all the precious days of youth in sin, and are now come to such a dreadful pass in blindness and hardness. And you, children, who are unconverted, do not you know that you are going down to hell, to bear the dreadful wrath of that God, who is now angry with you every day and every night? Will you be content to be the children of the devil, when so many other children in the land are converted, and are become the holy and happy children of the King of kings?

And let everyone that is yet out of Christ, and hanging over the pit of hell, whether they be old men and women, or middle-aged, or young people, or little children, now harken to the loud calls of God's word and providence. This acceptable year of the Lord, a day of such great favors to some, will doubtless be a day of as remarkable vengeance to others. Men's hearts harden, and their guilt increases apace at such a day as this, if they neglect their souls; and never was there so great danger of such persons being given up to hardness of heart and blindness of mind. God seems now to be hastily gathering in His elect in all parts of the land; and probably the greater part of adult persons that ever shall be saved will be brought in now in a little time, and that it will be as it was on the great outpouring of the Spirit upon the Jews in the apostles' days; the election will obtain, and the rest will be blinded. If this should be the case with you, you will eternally curse this day, and will curse the day that ever you [were] born, to see such a season of the pouring out of God's Spirit, and will wish that you had died and gone to hell before you had seen it. Now undoubtedly it is as it was in the days of John the Baptist; the ax is in an extraordinary manner laid at the root of the trees, that every tree which brings not forth good fruit may be hewn down and cast into the fire.

Therefore, let everyone that is out of Christ now awake and fly from the wrath to come. The wrath of Almighty God is now undoubtedly hanging over a great part of this congregation. Let everyone fly out of Sodom: "Haste and escape for your lives; look not behind you; escape to the mountain, lest you be consumed."

This sermon is in the public domain.

11

Anne Graham Lotz

THE RIGHT MAN IN THE RIGHT PLACE AT THE RIGHT TIME

═══════

Anne Graham Lotz has passionately carried the gospel throughout the world in venues ranging from downtown arenas to death-row prison cells, church sanctuaries to university lecture halls. She is the founder on AnGeL Ministries and the author of numerous books, including God's Story, Just Give Me Jesus, *and* Heaven: My Father's House. *The following sermon was delivered to the North Carolina Legislature on August 8, 2001.*

Father, we come before You and we thank You and praise You that You are Lord of the nations and You are Lord of this place and You are Lord of our hearts. You are the Creator of the universe who has leaned down out of heaven to speak to us through Your Word. And so as Your Word is presented, we are asking that You would speak to us personally, practically, relevantly. We want Your Word to make a difference, Lord, when we go out of this place. We don't want to think the same or feel the same or have the same perspective. Change us so that we are more in line with You. We are asking that You come down and bless us. While we know that we don't deserve Your blessings, we ask for them boldly in the name of Jesus, and it's for His glory alone that we ask. Amen.

Several years ago, there was an intriguing cover story in *Time* about Captain Scott O'Grady. Captain O'Grady was an American Air Force pilot who was flying a mission over Eastern Europe for the United Nations when the Bosnians shot down his plane from underneath him. As his plane exploded, he was able to eject from the plane. His parachute opened, and as he was floating down under the crystal-blue sky, he looked down to the area where he was going to land. It was already crowded with enemy soldiers and townspeople—all angrily shaking their fists, waving their guns, and waiting to capture him the moment he landed. Captain Scott O'Grady saw them waiting, and instead of landing in the middle of them, he maneuvered his parachute and actually landed on the other side of a little grassy knoll. As he hit the dirt, he cut off his parachute, grabbed his battery-operated radio, rubbed dirt in his face, and dived underneath a bush. Within four minutes of his landing on the ground, the area swarmed with enemy soldiers and townspeople, all looking for Captain O'Grady. He remained motionless under the bush. The soldiers stabbed the bush with their bayonets, coming within inches of his nose, searching for him. For six days, Captain O'Grady was the subject of an intense enemy ground search. During the day he stayed underneath the bush. At night he crept out and sucked the dew off the grass. He ate the grass and he ate the ants. But after six days, he was starving. He was thirsty. He was terrified of imminent capture. He was lonely. He was desperate to get out. And for the last time, on June the eighth at 6:30 in the morning, he sent up a last radio signal. He knew his battery was going dead, and he would have the opportunity to send only one more signal in hopes of contacting the rescuers. So he sent up his last weak radio signal. At that particular moment one of his friends was circling in a plane over that particular place. The friend heard the radio signal and called in the rescue team. Within moments the helicopters roared into the vicinity. Captain O'Grady ran out from under the ground cover, dashed across the pasture, dived across the threshold of the nearest helicopter, and sobbed, *"Thank you. Thank you. Thank you for saving me."*

Captain O'Grady would still be lost—probably captured—possibly dead—if he had not had a friend who was in the right place, circling overhead at the same moment in time the radio signal went out, so that the signal was heard and the rescue was made. I want to talk with you today about being that kind of friend to others—a friend who is the right person in the right place at the right time.

About sixty-five years ago, there was a tent revival down in Charlotte led by Mordecai Hamm. An eighteen-year-old gangly high school kid went and was converted, saved, placed his faith in Jesus Christ, and went on to be the one we honor today, Billy Graham. I think Mordecai Hamm was the right man at the right time in the right place giving out the gospel, and, of course, my father heard it and received it. And I think—in many ways—my father has been the right man, in the right place, at the right time for many others.

Recently we heard the story about a shark attack down in Florida. A little boy was attacked in the Gulf waters. When the shark ripped off the boy's arm, his uncle wrestled the shark to shore. The child was whisked off in an ambulance as the uncle proceeded to kill the shark. Someone pulled the boy's arm from the shark's mouth, iced it down, and took it to the hospital. The surgeons reattached it, and from what I understand, the little boy is going to go back to school and live a pretty normal life. I would say that uncle was the right man in the right place at the right time.

The Bible talks of several characters in the same way. One is Queen Esther in the Old Testament. Queen Esther was someone who came into a strategic position in Persia as a young Israelite whose people were going to be massacred. Her uncle told her that as the new queen she was to take a stand and be used of God to save her people from the holocaust that was coming. When Mordecai, her uncle, made the statement to her, Esther was afraid and said she would lose her life if she took a stand. Mordecai replied, "You may lose your life—that is right—but if you don't do this, God will raise up somebody else. But it may be that God has placed you in the kingdom for such a time as this." In other words, Mordecai was saying that Esther could be the right person in the right place at the right time. But she would not know that until she made the choice to take a stand.

Another biblical character that was the right person in the right place at the right time was Noah. And it's his story that I would like to use as my text.

Reading from Genesis 6, verses 5 to 14:

The LORD saw how great man's wickedness on the earth had become, and that every inclination of the thoughts of his heart was only evil all the time. The LORD was grieved that he had made man on the earth, and his heart was filled with pain. So the LORD said, "I will wipe mankind, whom I have created, from the face of the earth. . . ." But Noah found favor in the eyes of the LORD . . . Noah was a righteous man, blameless among the people of his time, and he walked with God. Noah had three sons: Shem, Ham and Japheth.

Now the earth was corrupt in God's sight and was full of violence. God saw how corrupt the earth had become, for all the people on earth had corrupted their ways. So God said to Noah, "I am going to put an end to all people, for the earth is filled with violence because of them. I am surely going to destroy both them and the earth. So make yourself an ark." (NIV)

There are four points I want to bring out about a person who is the right person in the right place at the right time. Noah lived in a *wicked* world that was *watched* and *warned* by God—and Noah *walked* with God. Noah faced the equivalent of a worldwide holocaust, as devastating as an atomic explosion. But because he was the right person in the right place at the right time, God used Noah to spare the entire human race from extinction. Had Noah not been the right person in the right place at the right time, you and I wouldn't be here today.

First, the world Noah lived in was a wicked world. Verse 5 says that the Lord saw how great man's wickedness on the earth had become—that every inclination of the thoughts of his heart was only evil all the time. In Noah's world there was no wholesomeness, no goodness, no gentleness, no loveliness, no kindness, no righteousness, no justice, no holiness at all. And our world is similar. I was born and raised in Buncombe County. And in Buncombe County we weren't taught to be politically correct; we were taught to be truthful. And our truth was based on or measured by the Word of God. So I want to describe to you a wicked world as the Bible describes wickedness.

A wicked world is one in which the worship of other gods is cloaked in multiculturalism. . . . Where the rejection of the authoritative truth of God's Word is excused as moral pluralism. A wicked world is one in which an abomination before God is endorsed as an acceptable lifestyle. A wicked world is one in which the killing of the unborn is as common as a tooth extraction. . . . Where the killing of the elderly and the infirm is promoted as an act of mercy. . . . Where leaders care more about their approval rating than about their accountability before God. . . . Where the family unit is destroyed and God is stripped from the schools. . . . Where reliable standards of right and wrong and the time-honored values of our forefathers are mocked, ignored, defied, and rejected—all in the name of toleration. . . . Where the discipline of our children is neglected in the name of self-esteem…where our children are immersed in TV, movies, magazines, books, video games, Internet games that glorify sex and violence and even involve their participation in those things. A wicked world is one in which we wring our hands and wonder, *How in the world could children kill children? How in the world can young men go in and slaughter their classmates? How in the world could America spawn a generation of superpredators that haven't even reached their teenage years and have no concept of right and wrong?* God help us!

You and I are living in a wicked world—from God's perspective. And this gets more solemn because Noah's wicked world was also watched. In verse 5 the Lord *saw* how great man's wickedness had become. In verse 12 God *saw* how corrupt the earth had become. God was watching. He didn't miss anything then, and He doesn't miss a thing today. He doesn't need to watch CNN or FOX News or *Larry King Live* or read the newspaper. He doesn't need an FBI investigation. He doesn't need a congressional inquiry. He doesn't need the jury's verdict. He doesn't need a committee report. He knows exactly what is going on. He sees it firsthand. He sees it all. God is watching . . .

the deals behind closed doors
the whispers behind backs
the personal agendas that are hidden in political posturing
the abuse of power that is called political savvy
the destruction of the environment
spin doctors that misinform the public
preoccupation with perverted pleasure
the exploitation of the human body
the abuse of innocent children
spoiled goods that are sold as fresh
the dangerous chemicals that are labeled safe
covenants that are broken by a whim
truth that is exchanged for a lie

glory that is given to the obnoxious
honor that is given to the blasphemous
and the legalized acceptance of abomination.
He sees it all!

Genesis chapter 6 verse 6 says He saw it all and was grieved. And *grieve* is a love word, isn't it? You don't grieve over someone you don't love. Scripture tells us that the Lord was grieved and His heart was filled with pain. And if He looked at Noah's world and His heart was grieved and filled with pain, do you think He cares about our world today any less? The Bible says that God so loved the world, He didn't just create it and bring it into existence; *He died for it.* He loves the world. He sees the wickedness and His heart is broken.

So God is patient, the Bible says, because He wants all to come to repentance. He doesn't want anyone to perish. But listen to me. The lesson of Noah is that there is a limit to God's patience. At some point He draws the line. But before we step over the line, God, in His goodness and His love, lets us know we're getting close. And so He warns us. God warned Noah's wicked world that was being watched by God. Judgment was coming! Verse 7: "So the LORD said, 'I will wipe mankind, whom I have created, from the face of the earth.'" And He warned them. He wouldn't have warned them if they didn't have the opportunity to repent and get right with God and avert the judgment. But in this verse it is as though He was speaking to Himself. Nobody was listening. In our world today I believe with all my heart we are drawing close to that line that has been drawn. I believe with all my heart that God, in His love and mercy, is warning us . . . "*Repent! Judgment is coming!*"

How does He warn us today? He warns us through a message like this. He warns us through faithful pastors in the pulpit and Sunday school teachers and people you watch on TV and listen to on the radio. But in the Old Testament when people reached a point when they no longer listened to God's word or to the prophets, God spoke to them through disasters—like a locust plague or a flood or a fire or an invading army. He sought to capture their attention, calling them to *repent*! It was as though He grabbed them by the collar and said, "Look up here. Put your focus on Me. Get right with Me."

As I look back on our world, there is evidence also of God's warning. One warning in particular was dramatic. It was given when Princess Diana died tragically in a car accident in Paris. Within twenty minutes of her death, the whole world knew about it. Everyone was in mourning and was shocked—it was horrific! Within the same week, Mother Teresa of Calcutta, India, died. And again, the entire world mourned! Could it be that God was warning the world that it doesn't make any difference if you are young or old, if you are rich or poor, if you are beautiful or homely, because one day every single person is going to step into eternity and face the judgment of God. Was He using the timing of the deaths of those two world-renowned figures to warn the world, "Judgment is coming. Repent of your sin. Get ready to meet God"? If He was, I don't think the world was listening.

I remember being in Kenan Stadium at the University of North Carolina for a football game one fall. Sixty thousand people had gathered and were screaming and cheering for their team. In the third quarter one of the referees fell over backward and lay sprawled out on the field. Within moments medics ran out, stripped off his shirt, placed electrodes on his chest, and tried to jump-start his heart. The entire stadium was quiet. You could have heard a pin drop as we all knew we were watching a man fighting for his life. Finally the referee was carried off on a gurney and put into an ambulance. At that moment, I wondered, *If God wanted to warn sixty thousand people to get ready! You never know when judgment is coming; you never know when you are going to step into eternity and face God and give an account to Him for your life—what more dramatic or effective way could He have chosen?* But I don't think those in the stands were listening.

Recently, a North Carolina icon, Dale Earnhardt, was killed on the last curve of the last lap of his race. In the blink of an eye, Dale Earnhardt stepped into eternity. He didn't know he was going to die at that moment. He had been in many races and had been involved in many accidents. I'm sure he didn't intend to die. He must have thought he would live a long time and enjoy his honors and his accolades and his grandchildren, yet suddenly, he was face-to-face with God. Everyone in North Carolina was caught up in Dale Earnhardt's death. My own nephew mourned and didn't leave his house for three days. God speaks to us through personal and public situations like that, imploring us, "Wake up! Get right with Me before it's too late!"

In North Carolina during the past few years, we have experienced one hurricane after another, many of them breaking the record set by the previous one. Our state has been devastated not only by the strong winds, but also by the unbelievable flooding. We have had a white hurricane that dumped twenty-five inches of snow on us, then froze in place for over two weeks, stranding thousands in dangerous, life-threatening situations. We have had record-breaking droughts and killer pollution of our forests and rivers.

And I wonder, *Is God just warning us?* Are we losing His blessing? Are we coming close to crossing the line for the reasons I gave previously? Is He saying, "Look up here. Give Me your attention. Judgment is coming"? The Bible says it is appointed unto man once to die and then the judgment. So whether the judgment comes nationally or statewide through some disaster or crisis, I know that when we step into eternity, we face the judgment of God personally. And we never know when that moment is going to come.

So what do you and I do? Noah, in a wicked world that was watched and warned by God, walked with God. He knew his world was coming under judgment, and therefore the most important priority of his life was to spend time with God. In fact, it was because he spent time with God that he not only heard God's warning, but also knew how to heed it. As a result, he was the right man in the right place at the right time.

If you and I thought that our world was coming under judgment, which I believe it is for all the reasons previously stated, there is nothing more important than walking with God.

What does it mean to walk with God? Let me illustrate it. Every morning I get up early, and then at 6:30 two friends and I go out to one of the city parks where we walk for two to three miles. We have two rules when we walk, or we don't walk together. The first rule is that we have to walk at the same pace, and the second rule is that we have to walk in the same direction. And the same rules apply when you walk with God. You have to walk at His pace, which means step-by-step obedience to His Word, which you make the time to read on a daily basis; and you have to walk in His direction, which means the surrender of your will to His. You can't go off in a direction of your own, setting your own agendas or goals. You must submit to His purpose, which involves prayer as you seek to know His will.

The North Carolina Legislature needs men and women who will walk with God. Men and women who, every day, make the time to read the Bible so that they can obey God's commands and live by God's principles. We need men and women who will get on their knees to pray in order to find out what's on God's mind and what His will is. If you say, "Anne, you have no idea how busy I am," I understand. I've never had the time to read my Bible, never had the time to pray. I have to *make* the time. Just like an appointment that I put on my calendar. Would you make time for God every day, spending time reading His Word and spending time in prayer?

Noah was a very busy person. He was a family man who had at least three sons. We know from the New Testament that he was in lay ministry, because he was a preacher of righteousness. And we know that he worked to build the ark, which was the size of an ocean liner—a job that took him 120 years. Yet he still made the time to walk with God. Aren't we glad? Because it was as he walked with God that God revealed to Noah what was on His mind. God said to Noah, "I am going to put an end to all people, for the earth is filled with violence because of them. I am surely going to destroy both them and the earth." When Noah walked with God, he discovered that what was on the mind of God was judgment.

I don't walk with God as closely as I would like, as consistently as I would like, as faithfully as I would like—but I do read my Bible and pray. And I believe that judgment is on the mind of God. He looks out at our world today and all of its wickedness and its corruption and its greed and its selfishness and its sinfulness; He looks at the world committing the greatest sin of all, which is just neglecting God . . . Turning our backs on God . . . Having nothing to do with God . . . Having no time for God . . . No thought for God. And judgment is on His mind! But there is something else on God's mind also. And it is the same thing that Noah discovered as he continued walking with God.

As Noah kept walking, God said, "Noah, make yourself an ark." In other words, not only was judgment on the mind of God, but salvation from judgment was also on His mind. And salvation from judgment is on God's mind today.

I believe if we continue on the path we are on, we are going to cross the line of God's patience and judgment will fall on us as a nation and as a state. But God has promised in 2 Chronicles 7:14, "If My people who are called by My name will humble themselves, and pray and seek My face, and turn from their wicked ways, then I will hear from heaven, and will forgive their sin and heal their land" (NKJV). The greatest benefit to our state and to our nation would be for us to humble ourselves, repent of our sins, and pray.

Noah, living in a wicked, watched, warned world, walked with God. As he walked with God, he discovered that what was on the mind of God was judgment and salvation. As he spent time walking with God, God told him exactly how to be delivered from that judgment.

God has also told us exactly how to be delivered from the personal judgment that awaits us in eternity. To escape His wrath for your sin, you must confess that you are a sinner (Romans 3:23; 6:23) and be willing to repent, or to stop deliberately sinning (Acts 2:38). You must ask God to forgive you (1 John 1:9) and place your faith in Jesus Christ as your Savior (John 3:16). You must believe that Jesus rose from the dead to give you eternal life (Romans 10:9–10), and you must invite Him to come into your heart (John 1:12; Revelation 3:20). If you follow these steps, making the conscious decision to confess your sin and claim Jesus as your Savior, it's as though you step into the "ark" and you are safe from God's judgment. Forever! When have you stepped from outside to inside the safety of God's ark? There is no other refuge from the storm of God's judgment that is coming.

God told Noah exactly what he had to do also to escape the judgment that was coming on his world. He was to build an ark according to God's specifications, then take on board pairs of animals from every known species that had breath.

I don't believe that Noah was a carpenter. I know he wasn't a zookeeper. I know he had never seen a big body of water. He had never even seen rain. But God gave him the wisdom to know exactly how to handle the crisis that confronted him. As a result, the entire human race was saved from annihilation.

And I believe God has a solution to the crises that face America—not only the practical problems that can seem overwhelming, but also the moral and spiritual crises that are a crisis of our spirits. But in order to know what the solution is, you and I must—it's not an option—we *must* walk with God. If we do, then we have the opportunity to be the right person in the right place at the right time, providing the solution for others who desperately need it.

I believe that God's eyes are searching back and forth over the whole earth, looking for those who would be willing to stand up and be the right persons in the right place at the right time. Men and women who, in the midst of all the busyness and wickedness and sinfulness, make the time to walk with God. Would you choose to be the right person in the right place at the right time? Would you choose now, as you live in a wicked, watched, and warned world, to walk with God?

Used by permission of Anne Graham Lotz.

12

Jesus—Savior of the World

THE PARABLE OF THE SOWER

On the same day Jesus went out of the house and sat by the sea. And great multitudes were gathered together to Him, so that He got into a boat and sat; and the whole multitude stood on the shore. Then He spoke many things to them in parables, saying: "Behold, a sower went out to sow. And as he sowed, some seed fell by the wayside; and the birds came and devoured them. Some fell on stony places, where they did not have much earth; and they immediately sprang up because they had no depth of earth. But when the sun was up they were scorched, and because they had no root they withered away. And some fell among thorns, and the thorns sprang up and choked them. But others fell on good ground and yielded a crop: some a hundredfold, some sixty, some thirty. He who has ears to hear, let him hear!"

And the disciples came and said to Him, "Why do You speak to them in parables?" He answered and said to them, "Because it has been given to you to know the mysteries of the kingdom of heaven, but to them it has not been given. For whoever has, to him more will be given, and he will have abundance; but whoever does not have, even what he has will be taken away from him. Therefore I speak to them in parables, because seeing they do not see, and hearing they do not hear, nor do they understand. And in them the prophecy of Isaiah is fulfilled, which says:

'Hearing you will hear and shall not understand,
And seeing you will see and not perceive;
For the hearts of this people have grown dull.
Their ears are hard of hearing,
And their eyes they have closed,
Lest they should see with their eyes and hear with their ears,
Lest they should understand with their hearts and turn,
So that I should heal them.'

"But blessed are your eyes for they see, and your ears for they hear; for assuredly, I say to you that many prophets and righteous men desired to see what you see, and did not see it, and to hear what you hear, and did not hear it.

"Therefore hear the parable of the sower: When anyone hears the word of the kingdom, and does not understand it, then the wicked one comes and snatches away what was sown in his heart. This is he who received seed by the wayside. But he who receives the seed on stony places, this is he who hears the word and immediately receives it with joy; yet he has no root in himself, but endures only for a while. For when tribulation or persecution arises because of the word, immediately he stumbles. Now he who received seed among the thorns is he who hears the word, and the cares of this world and the deceitfulness of riches choke the word, and he becomes unfruitful. But he who received seed on the good ground is he who hears the word and understands it, who indeed bears fruit and produces: some a hundredfold, some sixty, some thirty."

Matthew 13:1–23, NKJV.

13

John Stott

A Charge to a Man of God

John Stott (1921–) is a widely acclaimed preacher, author, and communicator of Scripture still serving at All Soul's Church in London, England. A hallmark of Stott's ministry has been his expository preaching. The following sermon was delivered in the Calvin Theological Seminary chapel on April 26, 2002.

1 Timothy 6:11–12

I want to talk to you about Timothy. I guess that you find him, as I do, a very congenial character. I have a very soft spot in my heart for Timothy. The reason is that he seems to be one of us in all our human frailty. Timothy was very far from being a stained-glass saint. A halo would not have fitted comfortably on his head. The evidence is there that he was a real human being like us with all the vulnerability which this implies.

For one thing he was still comparatively young when Paul wrote his first letter to Timothy. Probably by now he was in his thirties but still inexperienced for the heavy responsibilities that were being laid upon him. Another thing we know is that he was temperamentally shy. He needed to be reassured and encouraged, which is why the apostle Paul in one of his letters to the Corinthians urged the Corinthians to put Timothy at ease when he came among them. And then thirdly you will remember that he was physically infirm. He had a recurrent gastric problem, and for that reason Paul prescribed a little alcoholic medicine.

So that was Timothy—young, shy, and frail. But these are three handicaps. Three disabilities which are often found in men and women of God today. However, they endear him to us. Because of his weakness, we see in him a character who is similar to ourselves. And of course the power of Jesus Christ was exhibited in him, and His power was made perfect in Timothy's weakness as it had been in Paul's.

I wonder if anyone listening to me is like Timothy. You've been called to a responsible ministry of some kind for which you feel ill equipped. You are feeling inadequate for what it is to which God is calling you. Then I think Paul's words to Timothy are applicable to you as I've tried to apply them to myself.

Let's turn to 1 Timothy. "But you, O man of God, flee from all this [that is, the sins that he has been talking about] and instead pursue righteousness, godliness, faith, love, endurance and gentleness. Fight the good fight of the faith. Take hold of the eternal life to which you have been called when you made your good confession in the presence of many witnesses" (6:11–12)

You will notice Paul begins, "But as for you." This expression is found several times in both 1 and 2 Timothy. It indicates that Timothy was called to be different, as we are called to be different from the world around us: different from the prevailing culture. Timothy was not to drift with the stream. As Malcolm Muggeridge used to say, "Only dead fish drift with the stream"! He was not to drift. He was not to bend before the pressures of public opinion. He was not to be like a reed shaken with the wind. No, he must take his stand firmly for Jesus Christ, not like a reed, but like a rock in a mountain stream. For he was a *man of God*.

In the Old Testament this honorific title was reserved for people like Moses, David, Elijah, and other prophets. But in the New Testament the men or women of God were people who were mature in Jesus Christ and not just the giants that were dubbed men and women of God in the Old Testament. False teachers were men and women of the world. They derived their standards from the world around them. But men and women of God derived their values and standards from God Himself. And that's why Timothy was called to be—a man of God.

The Apostle now develops a threefold appeal to young Timothy— ethical, doctrinal, and experiential. These I think are still a composite appeal which the Scripture addresses to us today.

I. THE ETHICAL APPEAL

First we look at the ethical appeal. Verse 11 says, "Flee from all this and pursue righteousness and godliness." You will notice what we are to flee from. The rest of 1 Timothy tells us: things like materialism, the love of money, a drug called covetousness, and all evils associated with it. In addition, Paul says elsewhere "we are to flee from youthful passions." Not only immorality, but selfish ambition, indiscipline, and impetuosity, which we associate with you. So Timothy was to flee from these things.

What was he to pursue? Well, this is spelled out in six words. First, you'll notice them in verse 11, "righteousness and godliness." Righteousness is right dealing with our neighbor; godliness is a right relationship to God. *Eusebia* is the worship of God. Then he goes on to "faith and love." Faith is confidence in God; love is the service of other people. And then "endurance and gentleness." Endurance is patience with difficult circumstances, and gentleness is patience with difficult people. They are two different kinds of patience which are required of us as we seek to follow Jesus Christ.

What beautiful qualities these six things are: righteousness and godliness, faith and love, and endurance and gentleness! These six things remind us of the fruit of the Spirit. They also remind us and seem to be a portrait of our Lord Jesus Christ Himself. But what to me is specially noteworthy in Paul's ethical appeal to Timothy is that it is in two parts—negative and positive. These complement one another.

Negatively he was to flee from all evil, and positively Timothy was to pursue righteousness and godliness and all the rest. But simply, we are to run away from evil and to run after righteousness.

Now we human beings are great runners. We run away from anything which seems to be a threat to us. We run away from dander, which on the whole is a sensible thing to do. But we also run away from issues that we dare not face, from responsibilities that we dare not shoulder. And the word we use for that kind of running away is *escapism*. Instead, Paul says we are to run away from what is evil.

Positively we tend to run after whatever attracts us. Human beings run after pleasure; they run after success. They run after fame, wealth, power, and many other things. Instead, Paul seems to say, "How about running after righteousness? How about running after godliness and love and gentleness and endurance?" These are things that we ought to run after.

There is no passivity in the attainment of biblical holiness. We don't just sit there and do nothing, waiting for God to do it all. On the contrary, we have to run. We have to run away from what is evil and run after what is good and righteous. So the Apostle gives us no particular "holiness secret" to learn. He gives Timothy no particular technique to master, no particular formula to recite or button to push. There is nothing of that kind in Paul's teaching. Instead, we have to learn to run for our lives. As soon as we identify something as evil and displeasing to

God, we take to our heels and run. The one thing we must not do is to linger in the presence of evil or to "dillydally" with it. No, we are to get away from evil as fast as we can and as far as we can—like Joseph running away from Potiphar's wife when she tried to seduce him.

And then again, when we see something to be good, something to be pleasing to God and according to His will, then we must pursue it as we pursue those other things. We keep it in our sights; we "go" for it; we give it our minds, our energies, and all that is involved in running. So in the end the attainment of holiness is or should be extremely simple. We have to run from evil as we already run from danger, and we ought to run after righteousness as easily as we find it to run after success. That is the ethical appeal. We need to take it seriously as the Apostle calls us to be good runners.

2. THE DOCTRINAL APPEAL

Now we move on, secondly, to the doctrinal appeal. "Fight the good fight of the faith" (v. 12). It is almost certain that Paul is referring here not to faith without the definite article, although to be sure he has named it as one of the qualities we are to pursue (v. 11—faith and love). But in spite of that, it is almost certainly "the" faith with the definite article which he is intending to refer to here. Over against the postmodern fashion that truth is purely subjective and that there is plurality of truths (that you have yours and I have mine, he has his and she has hers and they have theirs) in all three pastoral epistles both to Timothy and to Titus, Paul assures us that there is such a thing as a body of revealed doctrine. There is such a thing as truth. He gives it different names—the faith, the truth, the teaching, the tradition, the deposit. It is of course the teaching of the apostle Paul and his fellow apostles. But it is the same sacred deposit that has to be carefully guarded, protected, and proclaimed. Timothy must fight the good fight of the faith, defending it and protecting it with all his might. He must turn away from godless chatter.

I find it very significant that just as good and evil are contrasted with one another in verse 11, so truth and error are contrasted with one another in verse 20. In other words, in both the ethical and the doctrinal appeal Paul lays on Timothy—and so upon us—complementary responsibilities. Ethically, we are to run away from evil and to run after goodness. Doctrinally, we are to turn away from error and fight for the truth. And it is a fight to which we are called.

Nobody enjoys fighting, except perhaps those who are pugnacious by temperament. Fighting is an unpleasant business. It is always undignified, often bloody and dangerous. The same is true of fighting for the faith. It is distressful to a sensitive spirit. There is something sick about enjoying controversy. Nevertheless, this fight is called by the Apostle "the good fight." There is a goodness about it, a necessity about it, although it may be distasteful to us.

But the reason it has to be fought and cannot be avoided is because truth is sacred. The glory of God is involved in the fight for the truth, and the good of the church is also involved. The good fight has to be fought. When truth is imperiled, as it often is in the world and in the church today, there is a painful necessity before us to fight and defend it. Even the gentleness which we are to pursue according to the previous verse is not to stop us from fighting! Gentleness should characterize our manner and methods in fighting, but in spite of the fact that we are called to gentleness, we are also called to "fight the good fight of the faith." Don't shirk this unpleasant duty!

3. THE EXPERIENTIAL APPEAL

As we come to the third appeal, we move from ethics and doctrine to experience the experiential appeal. "Take hold of the eternal life to which you were called" (v. 12). So what is this eternal life to which he is referring?

You will perhaps have heard of the little girl who was asked to define eternal life and said, "Well, God gives us life, so now we're stuck with it." But that is not the meaning of eternal life. The important thing about eternal life is not its duration, that it lasts forever, but its quality. It is the life of the new age, the life of the kingdom of God. You will recall that Jesus himself defined it for us in John 17:3: "This is life eternal that they may know you, almighty God, and Jesus Christ whom you have sent." It is in the personal knowledge of God, a personal relationship with God, that eternal life is to be found.

Timothy has been called to it. Presumably there had been a private call but also a public one when he made the great confession at his baptism. So Paul says to Timothy, "You possess eternal life. It was given to you when you believed and when you were baptized. So now lay hold of it." Doesn't that strike you as strange? It is to be exhorted to lay hold of something he already possessed. Had he not been a Christian for many years? Yes, he had. Had he not received eternal life long ago, as a free gift—utterly free and absolutely undeserved? Yes, he had. Then why did Paul tell him to lay hold of what was already in his possession?

The answer is that it is possible to possess something without enjoying it to the full. The Greek word *epilambano* contains a hint of violence. It is used of the soldiers when they laid hold of Simon of Cyrene and compelled him to carry the cross. And it is used of the mob in Jerusalem when they dragged Paul outside the temple area. So Paul's appeal to Timothy was to seize hold of this eternal life that was already his own. He was to make it increasingly his own. He was to enjoy it, experience it to the full.

I wonder if you have ever heard of Louis Delcourt. He was a young French soldier during the First World War. But when he was

visiting his mother, he overstayed his leave, and fearing the disgrace of
returning to his regiment late, he decided to desert. He persuaded his
mother to lock him up in the attic of their home, and there she hid
him and fed him for twenty-one years. But in August 1937 his mother
died. So there was no chance now of his retaining his incognito and
remaining in hiding. So, pale and haggard, he staggered along to the
nearest gendarmerie where he gave himself up. There the gendarme
looked at him in utter incredulity and said to him, "Where have you
been that you haven't heard?" "Haven't heard what?" asked Louis.
"That the law of amnesty for all deserters was passed years ago."

Louis Delcourt had freedom, but he didn't enjoy it because he
didn't know he had it. It is the same with many Christian people today.
They have been set free by Jesus Christ, the world's supreme liberator.
But they are not always enjoying the freedom with which they have
been set free.

We have considered Paul's threefold appeal to men and women of
God. Ethical—to run away from evil and to run after goodness.
Doctrinal—to turn from error and fight for the faith. And experien-
tial—to lay hold of the eternal life which we have already received.

APPLICATION

I would like us to learn a couple of lessons from this threefold appeal
which I think it is important for me not to omit. First, I would like to
ask you to note the extreme relevance to our own day of this threefold
appeal. The postmodern mood is unfriendly to all universal absolutes,
as we know. Yet the Apostle seems to set before us here three absolute
goals. He seems to be saying that there is such a thing as goodness—
pursue it. There is such a thing as truth—fight for it. So you see his
addressing this very personal message to Timothy.

I pray that God will give us in the midst of the postmodern world an unashamed commitment to those three absolutes: what is *true*, what is *good*, and what is *real*. That is our threefold commitment according to Paul's appeal to us. Let's think about these things a little bit longer.

The Truth

First, the truth. I hope you are building up your library. I hope you know that reading is one of the most neglected of all means of grace. You know what the means of grace are—they are means by which the grace of God comes to us, namely in the reading of Scripture, in prayer, in the Lord's Supper, in public worship.

There are millions of people in the world who lack literacy. They cannot read, and therefore they do not read. The tragedy is that we can read but we don't. There are many students in the universities who only read what they have to or maybe what they can find on their computer. I want to urge you, don't neglect reading.

In particular get hold of the great evangelical classics and read them. Don't be satisfied with modern evangelical melodrama! There are books which are more satisfying than that. I hope, seriously, you will build up a list of Christian classics and that you will determine to read those.

When Billy Graham was addressing some six hundred pastors in London, he said that if he had his ministry all over again, he would make two changes. The atmosphere was immediately electric. What? The great, world-renowned evangelist making changes in his ministry? What would he need to do? "Yes," he said. "If I had my life all over again, I would study three times as much as I have done."

Goodness

I am sure you know that in the twentieth century and the century before that, evangelical people were marked by their pursuit of holiness. They sometimes called it "practical holiness" as in the Keswick

Movement. They sometimes called it "scriptural holiness." But they were running after holiness. I don't see that in our evangelical constituencies today. Maybe there are some here, men and women, who will resolve by the grace of God to pursue, run after, holiness and Christlikeness. You know that God's great purpose for all of us is that we may be like Christ.

Eternal Life

And then there is laying hold of eternal life. Don't be frightened of experience. I myself believe that Pentecostal people are mistaken in making Christian experience a rigid stereotype of two stages. First, new birth or regeneration, and then baptism of the Holy Spirit. Nevertheless, I want to add that I believe in the second blessing . . . and the third and the fourth and the fifth and the sixth! I believe that after this mighty event at the beginning of the Christian life called "resurrection from the dead," the "new creation," there comes the process of sanctification during which there may be many deeper, richer, fuller experiences of God, the Father, Son, and Holy Spirit. We need to be pursuing goodness and truth and the experience of God.

A PLEA FOR BALANCE

I finish with the balance of this threefold appeal. That is to say, it incorporates within itself doctrine, ethics, and experience. Some Christians fight the good fight of the faith. They are great warriors for the truth. But they don't pursue goodness, let alone gentleness. Others are good and gentle, but they have no comparable concern to fight for the truth. Yet, others despise both doctrine and ethics and concentrate on their quest for religious experience. Why must we always polarize? We don't need to! All three of these are God's purpose for us. Oh, for balanced Christians!

Where are the Timothys of the twenty-first century? Are they here? I hope there are some here who will determine to hold fast to the truth, run after goodness, and take hold of eternal life. The church needs Timothys in the twenty-first century. They seek to be loyal not only to one or the other of these three goals, but to the whole biblical revelation, without picking and choosing what they happen to like. They pursue righteousness and fight the good fight of faith and lay hold of life simultaneously. These people are men and women of God and are fine exhibits of what I like to call BBC: Not the British Broadcasting Corporation! But rather, Balanced Biblical Christianity.

Used by permission of John Stott.

14

John Wesley

ON 1 CORINTHIANS 13

═══════════

John Wesley (1703–1791) was the founder of the Methodist Church and a lifelong opponent of the evil slave trade.

But earnestly desire the best gifts.
And yet I show to you a more excellent way.
—1 Corinthians 12:31 NKJV

I. Now, by the grace of God, we may choose the "more excellent way." Let us now compare this with the way wherein most Christians walk.

II. Surely there is "a more excellent way" of ordering our private devotions.

III. Christians usually apply themselves to their *business*, seeing it is impossible that an idle man can be a good man, sloth being inconsistent with religion.

IV. Every head of a family, before he sat down to eat and drink, ought to ask a blessing from God on what he was about to take and afterward return thanks to the Giver of all his blessings.

V. We need intervals of diversion from business of various kinds.

VI. What is the way wherein Christians employ money? And is there not "a more excellent way"?

1. In the preceding verses, St. Paul has been speaking of the extraordinary gifts of the Holy Ghost, such as healing the sick; prophesying (in the proper sense of the word; that is, foretelling things to come); speaking with strange tongues, such as the speaker had never learned; and the miraculous interpretation of tongues. And these gifts the Apostle allows to be desirable; yea, he exhorts the Corinthians, at least the teachers among them (to whom chiefly, if not solely, they were wont to be given in the first ages of the church), to *covet* them *earnestly*, that thereby they might be qualified to be more useful either to Christians or heathens. "And yet," says he, "I show unto you a more excellent way"; far more desirable than all these put together, inasmuch as it will infallibly lead you to happiness both in this world and in the world to come; whereas you might have all those gifts, yea, in the highest degree, and yet be miserable both in time and eternity.

2. It does not appear that these extraordinary gifts of the Holy Ghost were common in the church for more than two or three centuries. We seldom hear of them after that fatal period when the emperor Constantine called himself a Christian, and from a vain imagination of promoting the Christian cause thereby heaped riches, and power, and honor, upon the Christians in general; but in particular upon the Christian clergy. From this time they almost totally ceased; very few instances of the kind were found. The cause of this was not (as has been vulgarly supposed) "because there was no more occasion for them," because all the world was become Christian. This is a miserable mistake; not a twentieth part of it was then nominally Christian. The real cause was that "the love of many," almost of all Christians, so

called, was "waxed cold." The Christians had no more of the Spirit of Christ than the other heathens. The Son of Man, when He came to examine His church, could hardly "find faith upon earth." This was the real cause why the extraordinary gifts of the Holy Ghost were no longer to be found in the Christian church—because the Christians were turned heathens again, and had only a dead form left.

3. However, I would not at present speak of these, of the extraordinary gifts of the Holy Ghost, but of the ordinary; and these likewise we may "covet earnestly," in order to be more useful in our generation. With this view we may covet "the gift of *convincing speech*," in order to "sound the unbelieving heart"; and the gift of *persuasion,* to move the affections, as well as enlighten the understanding. We may covet *knowledge,* both of the Word and of the works of God, whether of providence or grace. We may desire a measure of that *faith* which, on particular occasions, wherein the glory of God or the happiness of men is nearly concerned, goes far beyond the power of natural causes. We may desire an easy elocution, a pleasing address, with resignation to the will of our Lord; yea, whatever would enable us, as we have opportunity, to be useful wherever we are. These gifts we may innocently desire: but there is "a more excellent way."

4. The way of love—of loving all men for God's sake, of humble, gentle, patient love—is that which the Apostle so admirably describes in the ensuing chapter. And without this, he assures us, all eloquence, all knowledge, all faith, all works, and all sufferings are of no more value in the sight of God than sounding brass or a rumbling cymbal, and are not of the least avail toward our eternal salvation. Without this, all we know, all we believe, all we do, all we suffer, will profit us nothing in the great day of accounts.

5. But at present I would take a different view of the text, and point out "a more excellent way" in another sense. It is the observation of an ancient writer that there have been from the beginning two

orders of Christians. The one lived an innocent life, conforming in all things, not sinful, to the customs and fashions of the world; doing many good works, abstaining from gross evils, and attending the ordinances of God. They endeavored, in general, to have a conscience void of offense in their outward behavior, but did not aim at any particular strictness, being in most things like their neighbors. The other sort of Christians not only abstained from all appearance of evil, were zealous of good works in every kind, and attended all the ordinances of God, but likewise used all diligence to attain the whole mind that was in Christ, and labored to walk, in every point, as their beloved Master. In order to [do] this they walked in a constant course of universal self-denial, trampling on every pleasure which they were not divinely conscious prepared them for taking pleasure in God. They took up their cross daily. They strove, they agonized without intermission, to enter in at the straight gate. This one thing they did: they spared no pains to arrive at the summit of Christian holiness; "leaving the first principles of the doctrine of Christ, to go on to perfection"; to "know all that love of God which passeth knowledge, and to be filled with all the fulness of God."

6. From long experience and observation, I am inclined to think that whoever finds redemption in the blood of Jesus, whoever is justified, has then the choice of walking in the higher or the lower path. I believe the Holy Spirit at that time sets before him "the more excellent way," and incites him to walk therein, to choose the narrowest path in the narrow way, to aspire after the heights and depths of holiness, after the entire image of God. But if he does not accept this offer, he insensibly declines into the lower order of Christians. He still goes on in what may be called a good way, serving God in his degree, and finds mercy in the close of life, through the blood of the covenant.

7. I would be far from quenching the smoking flax, from discouraging those that serve God in a low degree. But I could not wish

them to stop here: I would encourage them to come up higher; without thundering hell and damnation in their ears, without condemning the way wherein they were, telling them it is the way that leads to destruction, I will endeavour to point out to them what is in every respect "a more excellent way."

8. Let it be well remembered, I do not affirm that all who do not walk in this way are in the high road to hell. But this much I must affirm: they will not have so high a place in heaven as they would have had if they had chosen the better part. And will this be a small loss— the having so many fewer stars in your crown of glory? Will it be a little thing to have a lower place than you might have had in the kingdom of your Father? Certainly there will be no sorrow in heaven; there all tears will be wiped from our eyes; but if it were possible grief could enter there, we should grieve at that irreparable loss. Irreparable then, but not now. Now, by the grace of God, we may choose the "more excellent way." Let us now compare this, in a few particulars, with the way wherein most Christians walk.

I.

To begin at the beginning of the day. It is the manner of the generality of Christians, if they are not obliged to work for their living, to rise, particularly in winter, at eight or nine in the morning after having lain in bed eight or nine, if not more, hours. I do not say now (as I should have been very apt to do fifty years ago) that all who indulge themselves in this manner are in the way to hell. But neither can I say they are in the way to heaven, denying themselves, and taking up their cross daily. Sure I am, there is "a more excellent way" to promote health both of body and mind. From an observation of more than sixty years, I have learned that men in health require, at an average, from six to seven hours' sleep, and healthy women a little more, from seven to eight, in four-and-twenty hours. I know this quantity of sleep to be most advantageous to the body as well as the soul. It is preferable to any medicine which I have known, both for preventing and removing nervous disorders. It is, therefore, undoubtedly the most excellent way, in defiance of fashion and custom, to take just so much sleep as experience proves our nature to require; seeing this is indisputably most conducive both to bodily and spiritual health. And why should not you walk in this way? Because it is difficult? Nay, with men it is impossible. But all things are possible with God; and by his grace all things will be possible to you. Only continue instant in prayer, and you will find this not only possible, but easy: yea, and it will be far easier to rise early constantly than to do it sometimes. But then you must begin at the right end; if you rise early, you must sleep early. Impose it upon yourself, unless when something extraordinary occurs, to go to bed at a fixed hour. Then the difficulty of it will soon be over; but the advantage of it will remain forever.

II.

The generality of Christians, as soon as they rise, are accustomed to use some kind of *prayer*, and probably to use the same form still which they learned when they were eight or ten years old. Now I do not condemn those who proceed thus (though many do) as mocking God; though they have used the same form, without any variation, for twenty or thirty years together. But surely there is "a more excellent way" of ordering our private devotions. What if you were to follow the advice given by that great and good man, Mr. Law, on this subject? Consider both your outward and inward state, and vary your prayers accordingly. For instance: Suppose your outward state is prosperous; suppose you are in a state of health, ease, and plenty, having your lot cast among kind relations, good neighbors, and agreeable friends that love you and you them; then your outward state manifestly calls for praise and thanksgiving to God. On the other hand, if you are in a state of adversity; if God has laid trouble upon your loins; if you are in poverty, in want, in outward distress; if you are in any imminent danger; if you are in pain and sickness; then you are clearly called to pour out your soul before God in such prayer as is suited to your circumstances. In like manner you may suit your devotions to your inward state, the present state of your mind. Is your soul in heaviness, either from a sense of sin or through manifold temptations? Then let your prayer consist of such confessions, petitions, and supplications as are agreeable to your distressed situation of mind. On the contrary, is your soul in peace? Are you rejoicing in God? Are His consolations not small with you? Then say, with the psalmist: "Thou art my God, and I will [love] thee: thou art my God, I will [praise] thee" [Psalm 118:28 KJV]. You may, likewise, when you have time, add to your other devotions a little reading and meditation, and perhaps a psalm of praise —the natural effusion of a thankful heart. You must certainly see that this is "a more excellent way" than the poor dry form which you used before.

III.

1. The generality of Christians, after using some prayer, usually apply themselves to the *business* of their calling. Every man that has any pretense to be a Christian will not fail to do this; seeing it is impossible that an idle man can be a good man, sloth being inconsistent with religion. But with what view? For what end do you undertake and follow your worldly business? "To provide things necessary for myself and my family." It is a good answer as far as it goes; but it does not go far enough. For a Turk or a heathen goes so far, does his work for the very same ends. But a Christian may go abundantly farther: his end in all his labor is to please God; to do, not his own will, but the will of Him that sent him into the world—for this very purpose, to do the will of God on earth as angels do in heaven. He works for eternity. He "labours not for the meat that perisheth" (this is the

smallest part of his motive), "but for that which endureth to everlasting life." And is not this "a more excellent way"?

2. Again: In what *manner* do you transact your worldly business? I trust, with diligence, whatever your hand findeth to do, doing it with all your might; in justice, rendering to all their due, in every circumstance of life; yea, and in mercy, doing unto every man what you would he should do unto you. This is well. But a Christian is called to go still farther—to add piety to justice; to intermix prayer, especially the prayer of the heart, with all the labor of his hands. Without this all his diligence and justice only show him to be an honest heathen; and many there are who profess the Christian religion that go no farther than honest heathenism.

3. Yet again: in what *spirit* do you go through your business? In the spirit of the world, or the Spirit of Christ? I am afraid thousands of those who are called good Christians do not understand the question. If you act in the Spirit of Christ, you carry the end you at first proposed through all your work from first to last. You do everything in the spirit of sacrifice, giving up your will to the will of God; and continually aiming, not at ease, pleasure, or riches; not at anything "this short-enduring world can give"; but merely at the glory of God. Now can anyone deny that this is the most excellent way of pursuing worldly business?

IV.

1. But these tenements of clay which we bear about us require constant reparation, or they will sink into the earth from which they were taken, even sooner than nature requires. Daily food is necessary to prevent this, to repair the constant decays of nature. It was common in the heathen world when they were about to use this, to take meat or even drink, *libare pateram Jovi*; "to pour out a little to the honour of their god"; although the gods of the heathens were but devils, as the

Apostle justly observes. "It seems," says a late writer, "there was once some such custom as this in our own country. For we still frequently see a gentleman before he sits down to dinner in his own house, holding his hat before his face, and perhaps seeming to say something; though he generally does it in such a manner that no one can tell what he says." Now what if instead of this, every head of a family, before he sat down to eat and drink, either morning, noon, or night (for the reason of the thing is the same at every hour of the day), was seriously to ask a blessing from God on what he was about to take? Yea, and afterward, seriously to return thanks to the Giver of all his blessings? Would not this be "a more excellent way" than to use that dull farce which is worse than nothing; being, in reality, no other than mockery both of God and man?

2. As to the *quantity* of their food, good sort of men do not usually eat to excess. At least not so far as to make themselves sick with meat, or to intoxicate themselves with drink. And as to the manner of taking it, it is usually innocent, mixed with a little mirth, which is said to help digestion. So far, so good. And provided they take only that measure of plain, cheap, wholesome food, which most promotes health both of body and mind, there will be no cause of blame. Neither can I require you to take that advice of Mr. Herbert, though he was a good man:

> Take thy meat; think it dust; then eat a bit
> And say with all, Earth to earth I commit.

This is too melancholy: it does not suit with that cheerfulness which is highly proper at a Christian meal. Permit me to illustrate this subject with a little story. The king of France one day, pursuing the chase, outrode all his company, who after seeking him some time found him sitting in a cottage eating bread and cheese. Seeing them, he cried out: "Where have I lived all my time? I never before tasted so good food in my life!" "Sire," said one of them, "you never had so good sauce before; for you were never hungry." Now it is true, hunger is a good sauce; but there is one that is better still; that is, thankfulness. Sure that is the most agreeable food which is seasoned with this. And why should not yours at every meal? You need not then cast your eye on death, but receive every morsel as a pledge of life eternal. The Author of your being gives you in this food, not only a reprieve from death, but an earnest that in a little time "death shall be swallowed up in victory."

3. The time of taking our food is usually a time of *conversation* also, as it is natural to refresh our minds while we refresh our bodies. Let us consider a little in what manner the generality of Christians usually converse together. What are the ordinary subjects of their conversation? If it is harmless (as one would hope it is), if there be nothing in it profane, nothing immodest, nothing untrue, or unkind; if there be no talebearing, backbiting, or evil-speaking, they have reason to praise God for His restraining grace. But there is more than this implied in "ordering our conversation aright." In order to this it is needful, first, that "your communication," that is, discourse or conversation, "be good"; that it be materially good, on good subjects; not fluttering about anything that occurs; for what have you to do with courts and kings? It is not your business to fight over the wars, reform the state; unless when some remarkable event calls for the acknowledgment of the justice or mercy of God. We *must* indeed sometimes talk of worldly things; otherwise we may as well go out of the world. But it should only be so far as is needful; then we should return to a better subject. Secondly, let your conversation be "to the use of edifying"; calculated to edify either the speaker or the hearers, or both; to build them up, as each has particular need, either in faith, or love, or holiness. Thirdly, see that it not only gives entertainment, but, in one kind or other, "ministers grace to the hearers." Now is not this "a more excellent way" of conversing than the harmless way above-mentioned?

V.

1. We have seen what is the "more excellent way" of ordering our conversation, as well as our business. But we cannot be always intent upon business: Both our bodies and minds require some relaxation. We need intervals of diversion from business. It will be necessary to be very explicit upon this head, as it is a point which has been much misunderstood.

2. Diversions are of various kinds. Some are almost peculiar to men, as the sports of the field—hunting, shooting, fishing—wherein not many women (I should say, ladies) are concerned. Others are indifferently used by persons of both sexes; some of which are of a more public nature, as races, masquerades, plays, assemblies, balls. Others are chiefly used in private houses, as cards, dancing, and music; to which we may add the reading of plays, novels, romances, newspapers, and fashionable poetry.

3. Some diversions indeed which were formerly in great request are now fallen into disrepute. The nobility and gentry (in England at least) seem totally to disregard the once-fashionable diversion of hawking; and the vulgar themselves are no longer diverted by men hacking and hewing each other in pieces at broadsword. The noble game of quarterstaff, likewise, is now exercised by very few. Yea, cudgelling has lost its honor, even in Wales itself. Bearbaiting also is now very seldom seen, and bullbaiting not very often. And it seems cockfighting would totally cease in England, were it not for two or three right, honorable patrons.

4. It is not needful to say anything more of these foul *remains of Gothic barbarity* than that they are a reproach, not only to all religion, but even to human nature. One would not pass so severe censure on the sports of the field. Let those who have nothing better to do still run foxes and hares out of breath. Neither need much be said about horseraces, till some man of sense will undertake to defend them. It

seems a great deal more may be said in defense of seeing a serious tragedy. I could not do it with a clear conscience; at least not in an English theater, the sink of all profaneness and debauchery; but possibly others can. I cannot say quite so much for balls or assemblies, which are more reputable than masquerades, but must be allowed by all impartial persons to have exactly the same tendency. So undoubtedly have all public dancings. And the same tendency they must have, unless the same caution obtained among modern Christians which was observed among the ancient heathens. With them men and women never danced together, but always in separate rooms. This was always observed in ancient Greece, and for several ages at Rome, where a woman dancing in company with men would have at once been set down for a prostitute. Of playing at cards I say the same as of seeing plays. I could not do it with a clear conscience. But I am not obliged to pass sentences on those that are otherwise minded. I leave them to their own Master: to Him let them stand or fall.

5. But supposing these, as well as the reading of plays, novels, newspapers, and the like, to be quite innocent diversions; yet are there not more excellent ways of diverting themselves for those that love or fear God? Would men of fortune divert themselves in the open air? They may do it by cultivating and improving their lands, by planting their grounds, by laying out, carrying on, and perfecting their gardens and orchards. At other times they may visit and converse with the most serious and sensible of their neighbors; or they may visit the sick, the poor, the widows, and fatherless in their affliction. Do they desire to divert themselves in the house? They may read useful history, pious and elegant poetry, or several branches of natural philosophy. If you have time, you may divert yourself by music, and perhaps by philosophical experiments. But above all, when you have once learned the use of prayer, you will find that as

That which yields or fills
All space, the ambient air, wide interfused
Embraces round this florid earth;

so will this, till through every space of life it be interfused with all your
employments, and wherever you are, whatever you do, embrace you on
every side. Then you will be able to say boldly:

With me no melancholy void,
No moment lingers unemploy'd,
Or unimproved below:
My weariness of life is gone,
Who live to serve my God alone,
And only Jesus know.

VI.

One point only remains to be considered; that is, the use of money.
What is the way wherein the generality of Christians employ this?
And is there not "a more excellent way"?

1. The generality of Christians usually set apart something yearly—
perhaps a tenth or even one-eighth part of their income, whether it
arise from yearly revenue, or from trade—for charitable uses. Few I
have known who said like Zacchaeus, "Lord, the half of my goods I
give to the poor." Oh, that it would please God to multiply these
friends of mankind, these general benefactors!

2. Besides those who have a stated rule, there are thousands who
give large sums to the poor; especially when any striking instance of
distress is represented to them in lively colors.

3. I praise God for all of you who act in this manner. May you never
be weary of well-doing! May God restore what you give sevenfold into
your own bosom! But yet I show unto you a more excellent way.

4. You may consider yourself as one in whose hands the Proprietor of heaven and earth and all things therein has lodged a part of His goods, to be disposed of according to His direction. And His direction is that you should look upon yourself as one of a certain number of indigent persons who are to be provided for out of that portion of His goods wherewith you are entrusted. You have two advantages over the rest: the one, that "it is more blessed to give than to receive"; the other, that you are to serve yourself first, and others afterwards. This is the light wherein you are to see yourself and them. But to be more particular: first, if you have no family, after you have provided for yourself, give away all that remains; so that

Each Christmas your accounts may clear,
And wind your bottom round the year.

This was the practice of all the young men at Oxford who were called Methodists. For example: One of them had thirty pounds a year. He lived on twenty-eight and gave away forty shillings. The next year, receiving sixty pounds, he still lived on twenty-eight and gave away two-and-thirty. The third year he received ninety pounds and gave away sixty-two. The fourth year he received a hundred and twenty pounds. Still he lived as before on twenty-eight and gave to the poor ninety-two. Was not this "a more excellent way"? Secondly, if you have a family, seriously consider before God how much each member of it wants in order to have what is needful for life and godliness. And in general, do not allow them less, nor much more, than you allow yourself. Thirdly, this being done, fix your purpose to "gain no more." I charge you in the name of God, do not increase your substance! As it comes daily or yearly, so let it go: otherwise you "lay up treasures upon earth." And this our Lord as flatly forbids as murder and adultery. By doing it, therefore, you would "treasure up to yourselves wrath against the day of wrath and revelation of the righteous judgement of God."

5. But suppose it were not forbidden; how can you on principles of reason spend your money in a way which God may *possibly forgive*, instead of spending it in a manner which He will *certainly reward*? You will have no reward in heaven for what you *lay up*; you will, for what you *lay out*. Every pound you put into the earthly bank is sunk: it brings no interest above. But every pound you give to the poor is put into the bank of heaven. And it will bring glorious interest; yea, and such as will be accumulating to all eternity.

6. Who then is a wise man, and endued with knowledge among you? Let him resolve this day, this hour, this moment, the Lord assisting him, to choose in all the preceding particulars the "more excellent way." And let him steadily keep it, both with regard to sleep, prayer, work, food, conversation, and diversions; and particularly with regard to the employment of that important talent, money. Let *your* heart answer to the call of God, "From this moment, God being my helper, I will lay up no more treasure upon earth. This one thing I will do: I will lay up treasure in heaven; I will render unto God the things that are God's; I will give Him all my goods, and all my heart."

This document is from the Christian Classics Ethereal Library Web site [http://www.ccel.org/]. Edited by Edward Purkey, pastor, with corrections by George Lyons of the Wesley Center for Applied Theology; bracketed information added.

15

Billy Sunday

WHY DELAY YOUR REAL CONVERSION?

———————

Billy Sunday (1862–1935) was a professional baseball player from 1883 to 1891 for teams in Chicago, Pittsburgh, and Philadelphia. He was converted through the street preaching of Harry Monroe of the Pacific Garden Mission in Chicago. Sunday left a $5,000-a-year salary as a baseball player for $75 a month as an evangelist.

The following sermon is one of many preached by Billy Sunday, who was well known for his flamboyant, passionate delivery.

What does *converted* mean? It means completely changed. *Converted* is not synonymous with *reformed*. Reforms are from without—conversion from within. Conversion is a complete surrender to Jesus. It's a willingness to do what He wants you to do. Unless you have made a complete surrender and are doing His will, it will avail you nothing if you've reformed a thousand times and have your name on fifty church records.

Believe on the Lord Jesus Christ in your heart and confess Him with your mouth, and you will be saved. God is good. The plan of salvation is presented to you in two parts. Believe in your heart and confess with your mouth. Many of you here probably do believe. Why don't you confess? Now own up. The truth is that you have a yellow streak. Own up, businessmen, and businesswomen, and all of you others. Isn't it so? Haven't you got a little saffron? Brave old Elijah ran like a scared deer when he heard old Jezebel had said she would have his head, and he beat it. And he ran to Beersheba and lay down under a juniper tree and cried to the Lord to let him die. The Lord answered his prayer, but not in the way he expected. If He had let him die, he would have died with nothing but the wind moaning through the trees as his funeral dirge. But the Lord had something better for Elijah. He had a chariot of fire, and it swooped down and carried him into glory without his ever seeing death.

So He says He has something better for you—salvation if He can get you to see it. You've kept your church membership locked up. You've smiled at a smutty story. When God and the church were scoffed at, you never peeped, and when asked to stand up here, you've sneaked out the back way and beat it. You're afraid, and God despises a coward—a mutt. You cannot be converted by thinking so and sitting still.

Maybe you're a drunkard, an adulterer, a prostitute, a liar; won't admit you are lost; are proud. Maybe you're even proud you're not proud, and Jesus has a time of it.

Jesus said, "Come to Me," not to the church; to Me, not to a creed; to Me, not to a preacher; to Me, not to an evangelist; to Me, not to a priest; to Me, not to a pope; "Come to Me, and I will give you rest." Faith in Jesus Christ saves you, not faith in the church.

You can join church, pay your share of the preacher's salary, attend the services, teach Sunday school, return thanks, and do everything that would apparently stamp you as a Christian—even pray—but you won't ever be a Christian—until you do what God tells you to do.

That's the road, and that's the only one mapped out for you and for me. God treats all alike. He doesn't furnish one plan for the banker and another for the janitor who sweeps out the bank. He has the same plan for one that He has for another. It's the law—you may not approve of it, but that doesn't make any difference.

SALVATION A PERSONAL MATTER

The first thing to remember about being saved is that salvation is a personal matter. "Seek ye the Lord"—that means everyone must seek for himself. It won't do for the parent to seek for the children; it won't do for the children to seek for the parent. If you were sick, all the medicine I might take wouldn't do you any good. Salvation is a personal matter that no one else can do for you; you must attend to it yourself.

Some persons have lived manly or womanly lives, and they lack but one thing—open confession of the Lord Jesus Christ. Some men think that they must come to Him in a certain way—that they must be stirred by emotion or something like that.

Some people have a deeper conviction of sin before they are converted than after they are converted. With some it is the other way. Some know when they are converted and others don't.

Some people are emotional. Some are demonstrative. Some will cry easily. Some are cold and can't be moved to emotion. A man jumped up in a meeting and asked whether he could be saved when he hadn't shed a tear in forty years. Even as he spoke he began to shed tears. It's all a matter of how you're constituted. I am vehement, and I serve God with the same vehemence that I served the devil when I went down the line.

Some of you say that in order to accept Jesus you must have different surroundings. You think you could do it better in some other place. You can be saved where you are as well as anyplace on earth. I say, "My watch doesn't run. It needs new surroundings. I'll put it in this other pocket, or I'll put it here, or here on these flowers." It doesn't need new surroundings. It needs a new mainspring; and that's what the sinner needs. You need a new heart, not a new suit.

What can I do to keep out of hell? "Believe on the Lord Jesus Christ, and thou shalt be saved" [Acts 16:31 KJV].

The Philippian jailer was converted. He had put the disciples into the stocks when they came to the prison, but after his conversion he stooped down and washed the blood from their stripes.

Now leave God out of the proposition for a minute. Never mind about the new birth—that's His business. Jesus Christ became a man, bone of our bone, flesh of our flesh. He died on the cross for us, so that we might escape the penalty pronounced on us. Now never mind about anything but our part in salvation. Here it is: "Believe on the Lord Jesus Christ, and thou shalt be saved."

You say, "Mr. Sunday, the church is full of hypocrites." So's hell. I say to you if you don't want to go to hell and live with that whole bunch forever, come into the church, where you won't have to associate with them very long. There are no hypocrites in heaven.

You say, "Mr. Sunday, I can be a Christian and go to heaven without joining a church." Yes, and you can go to Europe without getting on board a steamer. The swimming's good—but the sharks are laying for fellows who take that route. I don't believe you. If a man is truly saved, he will hunt for a church right away.

You say, "It's so mysterious. I don't understand." You'll be surprised to find out how little you know. You plant a seed in the ground—that's your part. You don't understand how it grows. How God makes that seed grow is mysterious to you.

Some people think that they can't be converted unless they go down on their knees in the straw at a camp meeting, unless they pray all hours of the night, and all nights of the week, while some old brother storms heaven in prayer. Some think a man must lose sleep, must come down the aisle with a haggard look, and he must froth at the mouth and dance and shout. Some get it that way, and they don't think that the work I do is genuine unless conversions are made in the same way that they have got religion.

I want you to see what God put in black and white; that there can be a sound, thorough conversion in an instant; that man can be converted as quietly as the coming of day and never backslide. I do not find fault with the way other people get religion. What I want and preach is the fact that a man can be converted without any fuss.

If a man wants to shout and clap his hands in joy over his wife's conversion, or if a wife wants to cry when her husband is converted, I am not going to turn the hose on them, or put them in a straitjacket. When a man turns to God truly in conversion, I don't care what form his conversion takes. I wasn't converted that way, but I do not rush around and say, with gall and bitterness, that you are not saved because you did not get religion the way I did. If we all got religion in the same way, the devil might go to sleep with a regular Rip Van Winkle snooze and still be on the job.

Look at Nicodemus. You could never get a man with the temperament of Nicodemus near a camp meeting, to kneel down in the straw, or to shout and sing. He was a quiet, thoughtful, honest, sincere, and cautious man. He wanted to know the truth, and he was willing to walk in the light when he found it.

Look at the man at the pool of Bethesda. He was a big sinner and was in a lot of trouble which his sins had made for him. He had been in that condition for a long time. It didn't take him three minutes to say yes when the Lord spoke to him. See how quietly he was converted.

Matthew stood in the presence of Christ, and he realized what it would be to be without Christ, to be without hope, and it brought him to a quick decision. "And he arose, and followed him" [Matthew 9:9 KJV].

How long did that conversion take? How long did it take him to accept Christ after he had made up his mind? And you tell me you can't make an instant decision to please God? The decision of Matthew proves that you can. While he was sitting at his desk, he was not a disciple. The instant he arose he was. That move changed his attitude toward God. Then he ceased to do evil and commenced to do good. You can be converted just as quickly as Matthew was.

God says: "Let the wicked man forsake his way" [Isaiah 55:7 KJV]. The instant that is done, no matter if the man has been a lifelong sinner, he is safe. There is no need of struggling for hours—or for days—do it now. Who are you struggling with? Not God. God's mind was made up long before the foundations of the earth were laid. The plan of salvation was made long before there was any sin in the world. Electricity existed long before there was any car wheel for it to drive. "Let the wicked man forsake his way." When? Within a month, within a week, within a day, within an hour? No! Now! The instant you yield, God's plan of salvation is thrown into gear. You will be saved before you know it, like a child being born.

Rising and following Christ switched Matthew from the broad to the narrow way. He must have counted the cost as he would have balanced his cash book. He put one side against the other. The life he was living led to all chance of gain. On the other side there was Jesus, and Jesus outweighs all else. He saw the balance turn as the tide of a battle turns, and then it ended with his decision. The sinner died and the disciple was born.

I believe that the reason the story of Matthew was written was to show how a man could be converted quickly and quietly. It didn't take him five or ten years to begin to do something—he got busy right away.

You don't believe in quick conversions? There have been a dozen men of modern times who have been powers for God whose conversion was as quiet as Matthew's. Charles G. Finney never went to a camp meeting. He was out in the woods alone, praying, when he was converted. Sam Jones, a mighty man of God, was converted at the bedside of his dying father. Moody accepted Christ while waiting on a customer in a boot and shoe store. Dr. Chapman was converted as a boy in a Sunday school. All the other boys in the class had accepted Christ, and only Wilbur remained. The teacher turned to him and said, "And how about you, Wilbur?" He said, "I will," and he turned to Christ and has been one of His most powerful evangelists for many years. Gipsy Smith was converted in his father's tent. Torrey was an agnostic, and in comparing agnosticism, infidelity, and Christianity, he found the scale tipped toward Christ. Luther was converted as he crawled up a flight of stairs in Rome.

Seemingly the men who have moved the world for Christ have been converted in a quiet manner. The way to judge a tree is by its fruit. Judge a tree of quiet conversion in this way.

Another lesson. When conversion compels people to forsake their previous calling, God gives them a better job. Luke said, "He left all" [Luke 5:28 KJV]. Little did he [Matthew] dream that his influence would be world-reaching and eternity-covering. His position as tax collector seemed like a big job, but it was picking up pins compared to the job God gave him. Some of you may be holding back for fear of being put out of your job. If you do right, God will see that you do not suffer. He has given plenty of promises, and if you plant your feet on them, you can defy the poorhouse. Trust in the Lord means that God will feed you. Following Christ you may discover a gold mine of ability that you never dreamed of possessing. There was a saloon keeper, converted in a meeting at New Castle, who won hundreds of people to Christ by his testimony and his preaching.

You do not need to be in the church before the voice comes to you; you don't need to be reading the Bible; you don't need to be rich or poor or learned. Wherever Christ comes, follow. You may be converted while engaged in your daily business. Men cannot put up a wall and keep Jesus away. The still small voice will find you.

Right where the two roads through life diverge, God has put Calvary. There he put up a cross, the stumbling block over which the love of God said, "I'll touch the heart of man with the thought of father and son." He thought that would win the world to Him, but for nineteen hundred years men have climbed the Mount of Calvary and trampled into the earth the tenderest teachings of God.

You are on the devil's side. How are you going to cross over?

So you cross the line and God won't issue any extradition papers. Some of you want to cross. If you believe, then say so, and step across. I'll bet there are hundreds that are on the edge of the line and many are standing straddling it. But that won't save you. You believe in your heart—confess Him with your mouth. With his heart man believes, and with his mouth he confesses. Then confess and receive salvation, full, free, perfect, and external. God will not grant any extradition papers. Get over the old line. A man isn't a soldier because he wears a uniform, carries a gun, or carries a canteen. He is a soldier when he makes a definite enlistment. All of the others can be bought without enlisting. When a man becomes a soldier, he goes out on muster day and takes an oath to defend his country. It's the oath that makes him a soldier. Going to church doesn't make you a Christian any more than going to a garage makes you an automobile, but public definite enlistment for Christ makes you a Christian.

"Oh," a woman said to me out in Iowa, "Mr. Sunday, I don't think I have to confess with my mouth." I said: "You're putting up your thought against God's."

M-o-u-t-h doesn't spell *intellect*. It spells *mouth*, and you must confess with your mouth. The mouth is the biggest part about most people, anyhow.

What must I do?

Philosophy doesn't answer it. Infidelity doesn't answer it. First, "believe on the Lord Jesus Christ, and thou shalt be saved." Believe on the Lord. Lord—that's His kingly name. That's the name He reigns under. "Thou shalt call His name Jesus" [Matthew 1:21 KJV]. It takes that kind of a confession. Give me a Savior with a sympathetic eye to watch me so I shall not slander. Give me a Savior with a strong arm to catch me if I stumble. Give me a Savior that will hear my slightest moan.

Believe on the Lord Jesus Christ and be saved. Christ is His resurrection name. He is sitting at the right hand of the Father interceding for us.

Because of His divinity He understands God's side of it, and because of His humanity He understands our side of it. Who is better qualified to be the mediator? He's a mediator. What is that? A lawyer is a mediator between the jury and the defendant. A retail merchant is a mediator between the wholesale dealer and the consumer. Therefore, Jesus Christ is the mediator between God and man. Believe on the Lord. He's ruling today. Believe on the Lord Jesus. He died to save us. Believe on the Lord Jesus Christ. He's the Mediator.

Her Majesty Queen Victoria was traveling in Scotland when a storm came up, and she took refuge in a little hut of a Highlander. She stayed there for an hour, and when she went, the good wife said to her husband, "We'll tie a ribbon on that chair, because Her Majesty has sat on it, and no one else will ever sit on it." A friend of mine was there later and was going to sit in the chair when the man cried: "Nae, nae, mon. Dinna sit there. Her Majesty spent an hour with us once, and she sat on that chair, and we tied a ribbon on it, and no one else will ever sit on it." They were honored that Her Majesty had spent the hour with them. It brought unspeakable joy to them.

It's great that Jesus Christ will sit on the throne of my heart, not for an hour, but here to sway His power forever and ever.

"HE DIED FOR ME"

In the [Civil] war there was a band of [guerrillas]—[Quantrill's] band—that had been ordered to be shot on sight. They had burned a town in Iowa, and they had been caught. One long ditch was dug, and they were lined up in front of it and blindfolded and tied, and just as the firing squad was ready to present arms, a young man dashed through the bushes and cried, "Stop!" He told the commander of the firing squad that he was as guilty as any of the others, but he had escaped and had come of his own free will, and pointed to one man in the line and asked to take his place. "I'm single," he said, "while he has a wife and babies." The commander of that firing squad was an usher in one of the cities in which I held meetings, and he told me how the young fellow was blindfolded and bound and the guns rang out and he fell dead.

Time went on, and one day a man came upon another in a graveyard in Missouri, weeping and shaping the grave into form. The first man asked who was buried there, and the other said, "The best friend I ever had." Then he told how he had not gone far away but had come back and got the body of his friend after he had been shot and buried it; so he knew he had the right body. And he had brought a withered bouquet all the way from his home to put on the grave. He was poor then and could not afford anything costly, but he had placed a slab of wood on the pliable earth with these words on it: "He died for me."

Major Whittle stood by the grave some time later and saw the same monument. If you go there now, you will see something different. The man became rich, and today there is a marble monument fifteen feet high and on it this inscription:

SACRED TO THE MEMORY OF

WILLIE LEE

HE TOOK MY PLACE IN THE LINE

HE DIED FOR ME

Sacred to the memory of Jesus Christ. He took our place on the cross and gave His life that we might live and go to heaven and reign with Him.

"Believe on the Lord Jesus Christ, confess Him with thy mouth, and thou shalt be saved and thy house."

It is a great salvation that can reach down into the quagmire of filth, pull a young man out, and send him out to hunt [for] his mother and fill her days with sunshine. It is a great salvation, for it saves from great sin.

The way to salvation is not Harvard, Yale, Princeton, Vassar, or Wellesley. Environment and culture can't put you into heaven without you accept Jesus Christ.

It's great. I want to tell you that the way to heaven is a blood-stained way. No man has ever reached it without Jesus Christ, and he never will.

This sermon is in the public domain.

16

Pope John Paul II

EXCERPT FROM "RECONCILIATION AND PENANCE: IN THE MISSION OF THE CHURCH TODAY"

Pope John Paul II (Karol Wojtyla; 1920–2005) was elected pope on October 16, 1978, becoming the first non-Italian pope in more than 450 years. The following excerpt is from the Post-Synodal Apostolic Exhortation, which was delivered by Pope John Paul II to the bishops, clergy, and faithful on December 2, 1984.

1. To speak of reconciliation and penance is for the men and women of our time an invitation to rediscover, translated into their own way of speaking, the very words with which our Savior and Teacher Jesus Christ began His preaching: "Repent, and believe in the gospel,"[1] that is to say, accept the good news of love, of adoption as children of God and hence of brotherhood.

Why does the church put forward once more this subject and this invitation?

The concern to know better and to understand modern man and the contemporary world, to solve their puzzle and reveal their mystery, to discern the ferments of good and evil within them, has long caused many people to direct at man and the world a questioning gaze. It is the gaze of the historian and sociologist, philosopher and theologian, psychologist and humanist, poet and mystic: above all, it is the gaze, anxious yet full of hope, of the pastor.

In an exemplary fashion this is shown on every page of the important pastoral constitution of the Second Vatican Council *Gaudium et Spes* on the church in the modern world, particularly in its wide-ranging and penetrating introduction. It is likewise shown in certain documents issued through the wisdom and charity of my esteemed predecessors, whose admirable pontificates were marked by the historic and prophetic event of that ecumenical council.

In common with others, the pastor, too, can discern among the various unfortunate characteristics of the world and of humanity in our time the existence of many deep and painful divisions.

A SHATTERED WORLD

2. These divisions are seen in the relationships between individuals and groups, and also at the level of larger groups: nations against nations and blocs of opposing countries in headlong quest for domination. At the root of this alienation, it is not hard to discern conflicts which, instead of being resolved through dialogue, grow more acute in confrontation and opposition.

Careful observers, studying the elements that cause division, discover reasons of the most widely differing kinds: from the growing disproportion between groups, social classes, and countries to ideological rivalries that are far from dead; from the opposition between economic interests to political polarization; from tribal differences to discrimination for social and religious reasons. Moreover, certain facts that are obvious to all constitute as it were the pitiful face of the division for which they are the fruit and demonstrate its seriousness in an inescapably concrete way. Among the many other painful social phenomena of our times, one can note:

- The trampling upon the basic rights of the human person, the first of these being the right to life and to worthy quality of life, which is all the more scandalous in that it coexists with rhetoric never before known on these same rights.

- Hidden attacks and pressures against the freedom of individuals and groups, not excluding the freedom which is most offended against and threatened: the freedom to have, profess, and practice one's own faith.

- The various forms of discrimination: racial, cultural, religious, etc.

- Violence and terrorism.

- The use of torture and unjust and unlawful methods of repression.

- The stockpiling of conventional or atomic weapons; the arms race with the spending on military purposes of sums which could be used to alleviate the undeserved misery of people that are socially and economically depressed.

- An unfair distribution of the world's resources and of the assets of civilization, which reaches its highest point in a type of social organization whereby the distance between the human conditions of the rich and the poor become ever greater.[2] The overwhelming power of this division makes the world in which we live a world shattered[3] to its very foundations.

Moreover, the church—without identifying herself with the world or being of the world—is in the world and is engaged in dialogue with the world.[4] It is therefore not surprising if one notices in the structure of the church herself repercussions and signs of the division affecting human society. Over and above the divisions between the Christian communions that have afflicted her for centuries, the church today is experiencing within herself sporadic divisions among her own members, divisions caused by differing views of options in the doctrinal and pastoral field.[5] These divisions, too, can at times seem incurable.

However disturbing these divisions may seem at first sight, it is only by a careful examination that one can detect their root: it is to be found in a wound in man's inmost self. In the light of faith we call it sin: beginning with original sin, which all of us bear from birth as an inheritance from our first parents, to the sin which each one of us commits when we abuse our own freedom.

LONGING FOR RECONCILIATION

3. Nevertheless, the same inquiring gaze, if it is discerning enough, detects in the very midst of division an unmistakable desire among people of goodwill and true Christians to mend the division, to heal the wounds, and to reestablish at all levels an essential unity. This desire arouses in many people a real longing for reconciliation even in cases where there is no actual use of this word.

Some consider reconciliation as an impossible dream which ideally might become the lever for a true transformation of society. For others it is to be gained by arduous efforts and therefore a goal to be reached through serious reflection and action. Whatever the case, the longing for sincere and consistent reconciliation is without a shadow of doubt a fundamental driving force in our society, reflecting an irrepressible desire for peace. And it is as strongly so as the factors of division, even though this is a paradox.

But reconciliation cannot be less profound than the division itself. They long for reconciliation, and reconciliation itself will be complete and effective only to the extent that they reach—in order to heal it—that original wound which is the root of all other wounds: namely, sin.

THE SYNOD'S VIEW

4. Therefore, every institution or organization concerned with serving people and saving them in their fundamental dimensions must closely study reconciliation in order to grasp more fully its meaning and significance and in order to draw the necessary practical conclusions.

The church of Jesus Christ could not fail to make this study. With the devotion of a mother and the understanding of a teacher, she earnestly and carefully applies herself to detecting in society not only the signs of division but also the no less eloquent and significant signs of the quest for reconciliation. For she knows that she especially has been given the ability and assigned the mission to make known the true and profoundly religious meaning of reconciliation and its full scope. She is thereby already helping to clarify the essential terms of the question of unity and peace.

My predecessors constantly preached reconciliation and invited to reconciliation the whole of humanity and every section and portion of the human community that they saw wounded and divided.[6] And I myself, by an interior impulse which—I am certain—was obeying both an inspiration from on high and the appeals of humanity, decided to emphasize the subject of reconciliation and to do this in two ways, each of them solemn and exacting. In the first place, by convoking the Sixth General Assembly of the Synod of Bishops; in the second place, by making reconciliation the center of the Jubilee Year called to celebrate the 1,950th anniversary of the redemption.[7] Having to assign a theme to the synod, I found myself fully in accord with the one suggested by many of my brothers in the episcopate, namely, the fruitful theme of reconciliation in close connection with the theme of penance.[8]

The term and the very concept of penance are very complex. If we link penance with the *metanoia* which the synoptics refer to, it means the inmost change of heart under the influence of the Word of God and in the perspective of the kingdom.[9] But penance also means changing one's life in harmony with the change of heart, and in this sense doing penance is completed by bringing forth fruits worthy of penance:[10] it is one's whole existence that becomes penitential, that is to say, directed toward a continuous striving for what is better. But doing penance is something authentic and effective only if it is translated into deeds and acts of penance. In this sense penance means, in the Christian theological and spiritual vocabulary, asceticism, that is to say, the concrete daily effort of a person, supported by God's grace, to lose his or her own life for Christ as the only means of gaining it;[11] an effort to overcome in oneself what is of the flesh in order that what is spiritual[12] put off the old man and put on the new;[13] an effort to rise from the things of here to the things of above, where Christ is.[14] Penance is therefore a conversion that passes from the heart to deeds and then to the Christian's whole life.

In each of these meanings penance is closely connected with reconciliation, for reconciliation with God, with oneself, and with others implies overcoming that radical break which is sin. And this is achieved only through the interior transformation of conversion which bears fruit in a person's life through acts of penance.

The basic document of the synod (also called the *lineamenta*), which was prepared with the sole purpose of presenting the theme while stressing certain fundamental aspects of it, enabled the ecclesial communities throughout the world to reflect for almost two years on these aspects of a question—that of conversion and reconciliation—which concerns everyone. It also enabled them to draw from it a fresh impulse for the Christian life and apostolate. That reflection was further deepened in the more immediate preparation for the work of the synod, thanks to the *instrumentum laboris* which was sent in due course to the bishops and their collaborators. After that, the synod fathers, assisted by all those called to attend the actual sessions, spent a whole month assiduously dealing with the theme itself and with the numerous and varied questions connected with it. There emerged from the discussions, from the common study, and from the diligent and accurate work done a large and precious treasure which the final *propositiones* sum up in their essence.

The synod's view does not ignore the acts of reconciliation (some of which pass almost unobserved in their daily ordinariness) which, though in differing degrees, serve to resolve the many tensions, to overcome the many conflicts, to conquer the divisions both large and small by restoring unity. But the synod's main concern was to discover in the depth of these scattered acts the hidden root—reconciliation, so to speak, "at the source," which takes place in people's hearts and minds.

The church's charism and likewise her unique nature vis-à-vis reconciliation, at whatever level it needs to be achieved, lie in the fact that she always goes back to that reconciliation at the source. For by reason of her essential mission, the church feels an obligation to go to the roots of that original wound of sin in order to bring healing and to re-establish, so to speak, an equally original reconciliation which will be the effective principle of all true reconciliation. This is the reconciliation which the church had in mind and which she put forward through the synod.

Sacred Scripture speaks to us of this reconciliation, inviting us to make every effort to attain it.[15] But Scripture also tells us that it is above all a merciful gift of God to humanity.[16] The history of salvation—the salvation of the whole of humanity as well as of every human being of whatever period—is the wonderful history of reconciliation: the reconciliation whereby God, as Father, in the blood and the cross of His Son made man, reconciles the world to Himself, and thus brings into being a new family of those who have been reconciled.

Reconciliation becomes necessary because there has been the break of sin from which derive all the other forms of break within man and about him. Reconciliation, therefore, in order to be complete necessarily requires liberation from sin, which is to be rejected in its deepest roots. Thus a close internal link unites conversion and reconciliation. It is impossible to split these two realities or to speak of one and say nothing of the other.

The synod at the same time spoke about the reconciliation of the whole human family and of the conversion of the heart of every individual, of his or her return to God. It did so because it wished to recognize and proclaim the fact that there can be no union among people without an internal change in each individual. Personal conversion is the necessary path to harmony between individuals.[17] When the church proclaims the good news of reconciliation or proposes achieving it through the sacraments, she is exercising a truly prophetic role, condemning the evils of man in their infected sours, showing the root of divisions, and bringing hope in the possibility of overcoming tensions and conflict and reaching brotherhood, concord, and peace at all levels and in all sections of human society. She is changing a historical condition of hatred and violence into a civilization of love. She is offering to everyone the evangelical and sacramental principle of that reconciliation at the source, from which comes every other gesture or act of reconciliation, also at the social level.

It is this reconciliation, the result of conversion, which is dealt with in the present apostolic exhortation. For, as happened at the end of the three previous assemblies of the synod, this time, too, the fathers who had taken part presented the conclusions of the synod's work to the bishop of Rome, the universal pastor of the church and the head of the College of Bishops, in his capacity as president of the synod. I accepted as serious and welcome duty of my ministry the task of drawing from the enormous abundance of the synod in order to offer the people of God, as the fruit of the same synod, a doctrinal and pastoral message on the subject of penance and reconciliation. In the first part I shall speak of the church in carrying out of her mission of reconciliation, in the work of the conversion of hearts in order to bring about a renewed embrace between man and God, man and his brother, man and the whole of creation. In the second part there will be indicated the radical cause of all wounds and division between people, and in the first place between people and God: namely, sin. Afterward I shall indicate the means that enable the church to promote and encourage full reconciliation between people and God and, as a consequence, of people with one another.

The document which I now entrust to the sons and daughters of the church and also to all those who, whether they are believers or not, look to the church with interest and sincerity, is meant to be a fitting response to what the synod asked of me. But it is also—and I wish to say this clearly as a duty to truth and justice—something produced by the synod itself. For the contents of these pages come from the synod: from its remote and immediate preparation, from the *instrumentum laboris*, from the interventions of the Synod Hall and the *circuli minores*, and especially from the sixty-three *propositiones*. Here we have the result of the joint work of the fathers, who included the representatives of Eastern churches, whose theological, spiritual, and liturgical heritage is so rich and venerable, also with regard to the subject that concerns us here. Furthermore, it was the Council of the Synod Secretariat which evaluated, in two important sessions, the results and orientations of the synod assembly just after it had ended, which highlighted the dynamics of the already-mentioned *propositiones* and which then indicated the lines considered most suitable for the preparation of the present document. I am grateful to all those who did this work, and in fidelity to my mission, I wish here to pass on the elements from the doctrinal and pastoral treasure of the synod which seem to me providential for people's lives at this magnificent yet difficult moment in history.

It is appropriate—and very significant—to do this while there remains fresh in people's minds the memory of the Holy Year, which was lived in the spirit of penance, conversion, and reconciliation. May this exhortation, entrusted to my brothers in the episcopate and to their collaborators, the priests and deacons, to men and women religious, and to all men and women of upright conscience, be a means of purification, enrichment, and deepening in personal faith. May it also be a leaven capable of encouraging the growth in the midst of the world of peace and brotherhood, hope and joy—values which spring from the gospel as it is accepted, meditated upon, and lived day by day after the example of Mary, mother of our Lord Jesus Christ, through whom it pleased God to reconcile all things to Himself.[18]

Used by permission

17

Dwight L. Moody

THE LORD'S WORK

═══════════════

D. L. Moody (1837–1899) was an American evangelist who founded the Moody Church, the Moody Bible Institute in Chicago, and the Colportage Association. The following sermon was delivered December 14, 1873, to a group of young men in Edinburgh, Scotland.

What men want in doing the Lord's work is (1) courage, (2) enthusiasm, (3) perseverance, (4) sympathy.

1. Courage. The man who is afraid, who holds down his head like a bulrush, is not the worker whom God will bless; but God gives courage to him whom He means to use. I have been all along with young men, and a great portion of my work these fifteen years has been among them, and I find that they generally fail for want of courage. There is any quantity of young men in Edinburgh just now whose lives are a blank to them, and who have not discovered that God sends us to do work for Him.

He can qualify them for that work. John Wesley said, "Give me thirty men of faith, and I shall storm the citadel of Satan and win it for Christ"; and he did it too.

Talk of Alexander being a great conqueror; he was nothing compared with that little man, Saul of Tarsus.

Once I had been fishing long, and caught nothing, and I almost got discouraged. My Sabbath services were barren one day, and I was greatly disheartened. My heart was down, and my head was down. In came a brother. "How does the work go on with you?" asked of a fellow worker. "Splendidly," he said. "Great blessing on Sabbath." I told him my state of mind. He said, "Did you ever study the life and character of Noah?" "Yes; I know it by heart." "Well," said he, "study it again." And I did so, and found in him wonderful courage. For one hundred and twenty years that the ark was building, he labored to get men to believe in God's righteousness. He did not get one, and I said, "What have I to be discouraged about after that?" So I went down to the prayer meeting, and a man behind me clasped me by the hand, and said, "Pray for me, for I am in great trouble." And I thought what would Noah have given for encouragement like that! And a man rose up, and told that a hundred young men had just come to Christ in a neighboring town. What would old Noah have said to that? One hundred and twenty years, and no fruit at all; and yet he had courage to go on preaching!

All at once the clouds were all gone from my mind. If you get discouraged, keep it to yourself; don't tell anyone about it; for you will just discourage others if you do. Be strong and very courageous if you would do anything for God.

2. Enthusiasm. We need more enthusiasm. The more we have the better. I have a great admiration for Garibaldi [who unified Italy in the 1870s], though I cannot, of course, approve of all his acts. When put in prison he said, "It were better that fifty Garibaldis should perish than that Rome should not be free." This was the cause getting above the man; that is what we want. We want to forget ourselves.

There are one hundred thousand men waiting now to be brought to Christ, to be invited to come to Him, and shall we hang back? Let us have enthusiasm.

This formalism that abounds at the present day is the worst *ism* of all—it is worse than all the infidelity and skepticism of the land.

I remember reading in some history of the ninth century of a young general who with only five hundred men came up against a king with twenty thousand. And the king sent to him to say that it was the height of folly to resist with his handful of men. The general called in one of his men, and said, "Take that sword and drive it to your heart." And the man took the weapon, and drove it to his heart, and fell dead. He said to another, "Leap into yonder chasm," and the man instantly obeyed. Then, turning to the messenger, he said, "Go back and tell your king that we have five hundred such men. We will die, but we will never surrender." The messenger returned, and his tale struck terror into the hearts of the king's soldiers, so that they fled like chaff before the wind.

God says, "One shall chase a thousand, and two put ten thousand to flight." Let us have confidence in God. When men are in earnest, they carry everything before them. The world don't read the Bible, but they read you and me.

3. Perseverance. The men who have been successful are not those who work by fits and starts, but three hundred and sixty-five days in the year. By the grace of God, these eighteen years I have been kept working for God. People complain how cold other people are: that is a sign that they are cold themselves. Keep your own heart warm, as if there were no other but you in the world. Keep working all the time at steady, constant work.

For the last eleven years I have not let a day pass without saying something to somebody of Christ. Make it a rule that never a day pass without speaking for Christ. People won't like it. If you are a living witness for Christ, it makes people mad against you. You will suffer persecution, and be spoken against, and yet they will send for such a man first when they are in trouble or on their deathbed.

The man that is popular with the world is not a friend of Jesus. You cannot serve two masters. The world hates Christ, and if you are a friend of the world, you cannot be a friend of His. You may be sure that something is wrong with you when everybody is your friend. Every man here can win souls for Christ.

The public houses in America are called "saloons." There is a hall with a bar, and behind, a dining room, and above, sleeping apartments, and in these saloons the young men congregate at night, and drink and gamble. There was a terribly wicked man who kept a saloon, whose children I was very anxious to draw to my Sabbath school. So one day I called on this man and said, "Mr. Bell, I want you to let your children come to the Sabbath school." He was terribly angry, said he did not believe in the Bible, school, or anything else, and ordered me to leave the house.

Soon after, I went down again and called on this man, and asked him to go to church, and again he was very angry. He said that he had not been at church for nineteen years, and would never go again, and he would rather see his boy a drunkard and his daughter a harlot than that they should attend the Sabbath school. A second time I was forced to leave the house.

Two or three days after, I called again, and he said, "Well, I guess you are a pretty good-natured sort of man, and different from the rest of Christians, or you would not come back"; so seeing him in a good humor, I asked him what he had to say against Christ, and if he had read His life: and he asked me what I had to say against Paine's "Age of Reason," and if I had read it. I said I had not read it, whereupon he said he would read the New Testament if I would read the "Age of Reason," to which I at once agreed, though he had the best bargain: and I did so. I did not like it much, and would not advise any person to read it.

I asked Mr. Bell to come to church, but he said they were all hypocrites that went to church. This he would do, however: I might come to his house if I liked, and preach. "Here, in this saloon?" "Yes! But look here, you are not to do all the talking"; he said that he and his friends would have their say as well as I. I agreed that they might have the first forty-five minutes, and I the last fifteen of the hour, which he thought fair, and that was settled.

The day came, and I went to keep my appointment, but I never in all my life met such a crowd as when on the day appointed I went to that saloon—such a collection of infidels, deists, and reprobates of all kinds I never saw before. Their oaths and language were horrible. Some of them seemed as if they had come on leave of absence from the pit. I never was so near hell before. They began to talk in the most blasphemous way; some thought one thing, some another; some believed there was a God—others not; some thought there was such a man as Jesus Christ—others that there never was; some didn't believe anything. They couldn't agree, contradicted each other, and very nearly came to fighting with one another before their time had expired.

I had brought down a little boy, an orphan, with me, and when I saw and heard such blasphemy, I thought I had done wrong to bring him there. When their time was up, I said that we Christians always began service with prayer to God. "Hold," said they. "Two must be agreed first." "Well, here are two of us." And so I prayed, and then the little boy did so, and I never heard a prayer like that in all my life. It seemed as if God was speaking through that little boy. With tears running down his cheeks, he besought God, for Christ's sake, to take pity on all these poor men; and that went to their very hearts. I heard sobs throughout the hall, and one infidel went out at this door and another at that; and Mr. Bell came up to me and said, "You can have my children, Mr. Moody." And the best friend that I have in Chicago today is that same Joshua Bell, and his son has come out for Christ and as a worker for Him.

There was a family which for fourteen years I had tried to draw to Christ, but they would not come, and I had almost given them up as hopeless. We have a custom on New Year's Day in America of calling on our friends and acquaintances, and wishing them the compliments of the season. Last New Year's Day I thought I should call on the old doctor, which I did, and I offered up just a short prayer. That week he and his wife came to Christ, and next week his son, and a few days after his daughter, and now the whole family are converted.

"*This one thing I do*," said Paul [Philippians 3:13 KJV]. He had received thirty-nine stripes, and if he had another thirty-nine stripes to receive, "*This one thing I do*," forgetting the things that "are behind, I press towards the mark." A terrible man he was—this man of one thing and one aim, and determined to go on doing it.

"To every man *his* work" (Mark 13:34 [KJV, emphasis added]). If blessing don't come this week, it will come the next; only persevere. Be of good courage; Christ will strengthen your heart.

4. Sympathy. To touch the hearts of men is needed too. Some men have courage, perseverance, and zeal, but their hearts are as cold as an icicle. Christ might have been born in a palace had He chosen, but poor men would have said He had not come for them; but He was born in a manger, lower than their own rank of life. The minister who speaks to people as if he were separate from them, that tells them what *they* should do, this and that, will not carry them with him. To speak to men from a higher platform is not the way to do them good. It should be what *we* do—we poor sinners, and you. The milk of human kindness is a great element in bringing souls to Christ.

We have, in Chicago, a meeting for strangers; and it is most blessed. Every Monday night, seventy-five to a hundred young men newly arrived in the city assemble to find friends. A young man coming from the country to a situation, or to college in town, feels very lonely. He walks the street, and has no one, of all the crowds, to speak to him, and he is miserable. That is the time when his heart is softest; then, if anyone speaks to him or shows him acts of kindness, he never forgets it. The devil watches for friendless youths like those; and the ensnaring paths of vice seem refuges from loneliness. Such a young man, walking along the street, sees a big brown paper pasted on a boarding, or at a railway station, or somewhere else, having painted on it, "Strangers' Meeting tonight. All strangers invited to attend." So he goes, and meets a kind look and words of friendship, and it is better to him than anything in the world.

During our [civil] war, there was a Southern man who came over to a Wisconsin regiment, saying he could not fight to uphold slavery. Some time after, the mail from the north came in, and all the men got letters from their relations, and universal joy prevailed. This Southern man said he wished he were dead; he was most unhappy, for there were no letters for him. His mother was dead, and his father and brothers would have shot him if they could, for going against them. This man's tent-mate was very sorry for his friend, and when he wrote to his mother in Wisconsin, he just told her all about it. His mother sat down and wrote to her son's friend. She called him her son, and spoke to him like a mother. She told him, when the war was over, that he must come to her, and that her home would be his. When the letter reached the regiment, the chaplain took it down to where this man was standing, and told him it was for him; but he said it was a mistake, that nobody would write to him; he had no friends; it must be for someone else. He was persuaded to open it, and when he read it, he felt such joy. He went down the lines, saying, "*I've got a mother!*" When afterwards the regiment was disbanded, and the men were returning to their homes, there was none who showed so much anxiety as this man to get to his mother in Wisconsin.

There are hundreds of young men who want mothers, and any kindness done to them will not lose its reward.

18

Martin Luther King Jr.

I Have a Dream

═══════════════

Martin Luther King Jr. (1929–1968) was a pastor and civil rights activist. King traveled more than six million miles and spoke more than twenty-five hundred times, appearing wherever there was injustice, protest, and action.

The following sermon was delivered on the steps of the Lincoln Memorial in Washington, D.C., on August 28, 1963.

Five score years ago, a great American, in whose symbolic shadow we stand, signed the Emancipation Proclamation. This momentous decree came as a great beacon light of hope to millions of Negro slaves who had been seared in the flames of withering injustice. It came as a joyous daybreak to end the long night of captivity. But one hundred years later, we must face the tragic fact that the Negro is still not free.

One hundred years later, the life of the Negro is still sadly crippled by the manacles of segregation and the chains of discrimination. One hundred years later, the Negro lives on a lonely island of poverty in the midst of a vast ocean of material prosperity. One hundred years later, the Negro is still languishing in the corners of American society and finds himself an exile in his own land.

So we have come here today to dramatize an appalling condition. In a sense we have come to our nation's capital to cash a check. When the architects of our republic wrote the magnificent words of the Constitution and the Declaration of Independence, they were signing a promissory note to which every American was to fall heir.

This note was a promise that all men would be guaranteed the inalienable rights of life, liberty, and the pursuit of happiness. It is obvious today that America has defaulted on this promissory note insofar as her citizens of color are concerned. Instead of honoring this sacred obligation, America has given the Negro people a bad check which has come back marked "Insufficient Funds." But we refuse to believe that the bank of justice is bankrupt. We refuse to believe that there are insufficient funds in the great vaults of opportunity of this nation.

So we have come to cash this check—a check that will give us upon demand the riches of freedom and the security of justice. We have also come to this hallowed spot to remind America of the fierce urgency of now. This is no time to engage in the luxury of cooling off or to take the tranquilizing drug of gradualism. Now is the time to rise from the dark and desolate valley of segregation to the sunlit path of racial justice. Now is the time to open the doors of opportunity to all of God's children. Now is the time to lift our nation from the quicksands of racial injustice to the solid rock of brotherhood.

It would be fatal for the nation to overlook the urgency of the moment and to underestimate the determination of the Negro. This sweltering summer of the Negro's legitimate discontent will not pass until there is an invigorating autumn of freedom and equality. Nineteen sixty-three is not an end, but a beginning. Those who hope that the Negro needed to blow off steam and will now be content will have a rude awakening if the nation returns to business as usual. There will be neither rest nor tranquility in America until the Negro is granted his citizenship rights.

The whirlwinds of revolt will continue to shake the foundations of our nation until the bright day of justice emerges. But there is something that I must say to my people who stand on the warm threshold which leads into the palace of justice. In the process of gaining our rightful place, we must not be guilty of wrongful deeds. Let us not seek to satisfy our thirst for freedom by drinking from the cup of bitterness and hatred.

We must forever conduct our struggle on the high plane of dignity and discipline. We must not allow our creative protest to degenerate into physical violence. Again and again we must rise to the majestic heights of meeting physical force with soul force.

The marvelous new militancy which has engulfed the Negro community must not lead us to distrust of all white people, for many of our white brothers, as evidenced by their presence here today, have come to realize that their destiny is tied up with our destiny and their freedom is inextricably bound to our freedom.

We cannot walk alone. And as we walk, we must make the pledge that we shall march ahead. We cannot turn back. There are those who are asking the devotees of civil rights, "When will you be satisfied?" We can never be satisfied as long as our bodies, heavy with the fatigue of travel, cannot gain lodging in the motels of the highways and the hotels of the cities. We cannot be satisfied as long as the Negro's basic mobility is from a smaller ghetto to a larger one. We can never be satisfied as long as a Negro in Mississippi cannot vote and a Negro in New York believes he has nothing for which to vote. No, no, we are not satisfied, and we will not be satisfied until justice rolls down like waters and righteousness like a mighty stream.

I am not unmindful that some of you have come here out of great trials and tribulations. Some of you have come fresh from narrow cells.

Some of you have come from areas where your quest for freedom left you battered by the storms of persecution and staggered by the winds of police brutality. You have been the veterans of creative suffering. Continue to work with the faith that unearned suffering is redemptive.

Go back to Mississippi, go back to Alabama, go back to Georgia, go back to Louisiana, go back to the slums and ghettos of our northern cities, knowing that somehow this situation can and will be changed. Let us not wallow in the valley of despair. I say to you today, my friends, that in spite of the difficulties and frustrations of the moment, I still have a dream. It is a dream deeply rooted in the American dream.

I have a dream that one day this nation will rise up and live out the true meaning of its creed: "We hold these truths to be self-evident: that all men are created equal." I have a dream that one day on the red hills of Georgia the sons of former slaves and the sons of former slave-owners will be able to sit down together at a table of brotherhood. I have a dream that one day even the state of Mississippi, a desert state, sweltering with the heat of injustice and oppression, will be transformed into an oasis of freedom and justice. I have a dream that my four children will one day live in a nation where they will not be judged by the color of their skin but by the content of their character. I have a dream today.

I have a dream that one day the state of Alabama, whose governor's lips are presently dripping with the words of interposition and nullification, will be transformed into a situation where little black boys and black girls will be able to join hands with little white boys and white girls and walk together as sisters and brothers. I have a dream today. I have a dream that one day every valley shall be exalted, every hill and mountain shall be made low, the rough places will be made plain, and the crooked places will be made straight, and the glory of the Lord shall be revealed, and all flesh shall see it together. This is our hope. This is the faith with which I return to the South. With this faith we will be able to hew out of the mountain of despair a stone of hope. With this faith we will be able to transform the jangling discords of our nation into a beautiful symphony of brotherhood. With this faith we will be able to work together, to pray together, to struggle together, to go to jail together, to stand up for freedom together, knowing that we will be free one day.

This will be the day when all of God's children will be able to sing with a new meaning, "My country, 'tis of thee, sweet land of liberty, of thee I sing. Land where my fathers died, land of the pilgrims' pride, from every mountainside, let freedom ring." And if America is to be a great nation, this must become true. So let freedom ring from the prodigious hilltops of New Hampshire. Let freedom ring from the mighty mountains of New York. Let freedom ring from the heightening Alleghenies of Pennsylvania! Let freedom ring from the snow-capped Rockies of Colorado! Let freedom ring from the curvaceous peaks of California! But not only that; let freedom ring from Stone Mountain of Georgia! Let freedom ring from Lookout Mountain of Tennessee! Let freedom ring from every hill and every molehill of Mississippi. From every mountainside, let freedom ring.

When we let freedom ring, when we let it ring from every village and every hamlet, from every state and every city, we will be able to speed up that day when all of God's children, black men and white men, Jews and Gentiles, Protestants and Catholics, will be able to join hands and sing in the words of the old Negro spiritual, "Free at last! Free at last! Thank God Almighty, we are free at last!"

19

The Apostle Paul

SERMON IN ATHENS

═══════════

Paul then stood up in the meeting of the Areopagus and said: "Men of Athens! I see that in every way you are very religious. For as I walked around and looked carefully at your objects of worship, I even found an altar with this inscription: TO AN UNKNOWN GOD. Now what you worship as something unknown I am going to proclaim to you.

"The God who made the world and everything in it is the Lord of heaven and earth and does not live in temples built by hands. And he is not served by human hands, as if he needed anything, because he himself gives all men life and breath and everything else. From one man he made every nation of men, that they should inhabit the whole earth; and he determined the times set for them and the exact places where they should live. God did this so that men would seek him and perhaps reach out for him and find him, though he is not far from each one of us. 'For in him we live and move and have our being.' As some of your own poets have said, 'We are his offspring.'

"Therefore since we are God's offspring, we should not think that the divine being is like gold or silver or stone—an image made by man's design and skill. In the past God overlooked such ignorance, but now he commands all people everywhere to repent. For he has set a day when he will judge the world with justice by the man he has appointed. He has given proof of this to all men by raising him from the dead."

When they heard about the resurrection of the dead, some of them sneered, but others said, "We want to hear you again on this subject." At that, Paul left the Council.

Acts 17:22–23, NIV.

Notes

1. Mark 1:15 RSV.
2. Cf. Pope John Paul II, opening speech at the Third General Conference of Latin American Episcopate: AAS71 (1979), 198–204.
3. The idea of a "shattered world" is seen in the works of numerous contemporary writers, both Christian and non-Christian, witnesses of man's condition in this tormented period of history.
4. Cf. Pastoral Constitution on the Church in the Modern World *Gaudium et Spes*, 3, 43, and 44: Decree on the Ministry and Life of Priests *Presbyterorum Ordinis*, 12: Pope Paul VI, encyclical Eccelsiam Suam: AAS 56 (1964): 609–59.
5. At the very beginning of the church, the apostle Paul wrote with words of fire about division in the body of the church, in the famous passage 1 Corinthians 1:10–16. Years later, St. Clement of Rome was also to write to the Corinthians, to condemn the wounds inside that community: cf. Letter to the Corinthians, II–VI; LVII: *Patres Apostolici*, ed. Funk, I, 103–9; 171–73. We know that from the earliest fathers onward, Christ's seamless robe, which the soldiers did not divide, became an image of the church's unity: cf. St. Cyprian, *De Ecclesiae Catholicae Unitate*,

7:CCL 3/1, 254f.; St. Augustine, *In Ioannis Evangelium Tractatus*, 118, 4. CCL 36, 656f.; St. Bede the Venerable, *In Marci Evangelium Expositio*, IV, 15: CCL 120, 630 *In Lucae Evangelium Expositio*, VI, 23:CCL 120, 403; in *S. Ioannis Evangelium Expositio*, 19:PL 92, 911f.

6. The encyclical Pacem in Terris, John XXIII's spiritual testament, is often considered a "social document" and even a "political message."

7. As I wrote in the bull of indiction of the Jubilee Year of the Redemption: "This special time, when all Christians are called upon to realize more profoundly their vocation to reconciliation with the Father in the Son, will only reach its full achievement if it leads to a fresh commitment by each and every person to the service of reconciliation, not only among all the disciples of Christ but also among all men and women": bull *Aperite Prtas Redemtori*, 3: AAS 75 (1983): 93.

8. The theme of the synod was more precisely "Reconciliation and Penance in the Mission of the Church."

9. Cf. Matthew 4:17; Mark 1:15.

10. Cf. Luke 3:8.

11. Cf. Matthew 16:24–26; Mark 8:34–36; Luke 9:23–25.

12. Cf. Ephesians 4:23.

13. Cf. 1 Corinthians 3:1–20.

14. Cf. Colossians 3:1f.

15. "We beseech you on behalf of Christ, be reconciled to God" (2 Corinthians 5:20 RSV).

16. "We also rejoice in God through our Lord Jesus Christ, through whom we have now received our reconciliation" (Romans 5:11 RSV); cf. Colossians 1:20.

17. The Second Vatican Council noted: "The dichotomy affecting the modern world is, in fact, a symptom of the deeper dichotomy that is in man himself. He is the meeting point of many conflicting

forces. In his condition as a created being he is subject to a thousand shortcomings, but feels untrammeled in his inclinations and destined for a higher form of life. Torn by a welter of anxieties he is compelled to choose between them and repudiate some among them. Worse still, feeble and sinful as he is, he often does the very thing he hates and does not do what he wants (cf Rom 7:14ff). And so he feels himself divided, and the result is a host of discords in social life." *Gaudium et Spes*, 10.

18. Cf. Colossians 1:19f.

Index